PROMOTING POSITIVE MENTAL HEALTH IN THE PRIMARY SCHOOL

Mental health and wellbeing is a hugely important agenda in education, both nationally and internationally. *Promoting Positive Mental Health in the Primary School* unpacks scientific and psychological research and evidence to explain positive mental health through the lens of a primary classroom in the language of teaching professionals.

Chapter by chapter, the book focuses on specific elements fundamental to positive mental health promotion in the classroom, including developing positive relationships, emotional literacy and empowering children as learners as well as the importance of teacher wellbeing, and illustrates how these can be achieved. It offers:

- an examination into the connection between positive mental health and good teaching,
- guidance underpinned by evidence for teachers and school leaders who wish to embed a consistent approach to positive mental health promotion,
- practical suggestions for whole-school professional learning.

Written from first-hand experience in both teaching and research, this accessible text makes positive mental health promotion meaningful to teachers, helping them build understanding and move from theory into practice. It is an essential resource for all practising teachers, trainee teachers, school support staff and school leaders.

Deborah Holt, formerly a primary school teacher and headteacher, is a lecturer and researcher of positive mental health promotion in education at the University of Edinburgh.

PROMOTING POSITIVE MENTAL HEALTH IN THE PRIMARY SCHOOL

Theory into Practice

Deborah Holt

Routledge
Taylor & Francis Group
LONDON AND NEW YORK

First published 2020
by Routledge
2 Park Square, Milton Park, Abingdon, Oxon OX14 4RN

and by Routledge
52 Vanderbilt Avenue, New York, NY 10017

Routledge is an imprint of the Taylor & Francis Group, an informa business

British Library Cataloguing-in-Publication Data
A catalogue record for this book is available from the British Library

Library of Congress Cataloging-in-Publication Data
A catalog record for this book has been requested

ISBN: 978-1-138-58723-6 (hbk)
ISBN: 978-1-138-58726-7 (pbk)
ISBN: 978-0-429-50405-1 (ebk)

Typeset in Interstate
by Apex CoVantage, LLC

For Niki

CONTENTS

ACKNOWLEDGEMENTS

I would like to thank Morag Crolla and Bridget Ali for their support and encouragement and Georgina Peters-Holt for her artistic contributions.

I am grateful to the teachers and pupils from so many primary schools situated across Scotland for answering my questions, welcoming our students and participating in my research. Particular thanks to Westruther and Channelkirk Primary Schools in the Scottish Borders for allowing me to pilot the audit.

INTRODUCTION

Positive mental health promotion in education is a current priority in many parts of the world. This text is based on research into teachers' perceptions of promoting positive mental health and research into social, emotional and mental health-promoting practice.

Positive mental health promotion is a fundamental part of the primary school teacher's role, and, consequently, this text explores the relationship between being a good teacher and positive mental health promotion. Whilst educators certainly need mental health specialists to help support children who have been diagnosed with severe mental health difficulties, positive mental health promotion for **all** children is something that **all** teachers have the responsibility, the skills and the experience to carry out.

The book is divided into three parts.

Part I Theoretical and contextual background

Chapter 1 discusses definitions of positive mental health with a focus on what this might look like in a primary school child. Chapter 2 explores approaches to positive mental health promotion. It presents a rationale for schools as crucial places in which to promote positive mental health and explores the teacher's role within this.

Part II How to promote positive mental health in school

Chapter 3 discusses the importance of positive relationships. It presents strategies and approaches that can be used to build and strengthen relationships in the classroom. This includes the teacher-pupil relationships, which are a fundamental contributor to positive mental health. In a similar way, Chapter 4 discusses the importance of ethos and presents approaches to creating a health-promoting ethos in the classroom or school. Chapter 5 explains the relationship between emotional literacy and positive mental health and offers ways for teachers to model emotional literacy and help children develop their own emotional literacy. Chapter 6 explores ways in which empowering children as learners can contribute to their positive mental health. Chapter 7 briefly explores the relationship between specific lessons and embedded practice.

Part III Strategies for developing whole-school approaches, including those to promote teacher wellbeing

Chapter 8 presents the importance of a whole-school approach to positive mental health promotion and offers ways in which to take promotion forward as a school through professional learning opportunities. The Appendix is intended to provide a practical resource that supports this chapter.

In the final chapter, Chapter 9, arguably the most import contributor to a health-promoting school is discussed - teacher wellbeing. In order to promote the positive mental health of pupils, the teachers and whole school staff also have to have positive mental health. This chapter reinforces and explains the importance of teacher wellbeing. It presents suggestions for supporting staff wellbeing.

A key aim of the text is to help teachers and other school staff see the links between their practice and positive mental health promotion. Primary school teachers' existing knowledge and skills are usually fundamental to health promotion. Teachers are specialists and can be the experts in classroom positive mental health promotion.

Part I
Theoretical and contextual background

1 What is positive mental health?

This chapter will look at definitions of positive mental health with particular consideration of the primary school context. It explores what the characteristics of a mentally healthy child might be; for example, their ability to have fun or their resilience. The issue of stigma associated with the term 'mental health' is explored and emphasis is placed on mental health as a continuum influenced by a range of factors, rather than as an illness. Whilst drawing from theory and recent research, the chapter is firmly based within the primary school context in order to make it most accessible to the busy teacher.

What is mental health?

No definition or discussion of mental health can be effective without addressing the elephant in the room: the misunderstanding or misuse of the term mental health. Recent high-profile discussion of mental health issues by celebrities and the media does reflect the beginning of a change in attitude and understanding towards mental health. However, it cannot be ignored that the term 'mental' was often used as an insult and that there was (and often still is) a shame associated with having mental health problems and a stigma attached to those who experience poor mental health.

There should be no stigma, and it is not possible to promote positive mental health if you have a deficit attitude towards mental illness or poor mental health. If we want to remove the perceptions of stigma and shame attached to mental health in our schools and classrooms, we need to increase understanding of mental health. Everyone has mental health just as they have physical health. Mental health, just like physical health, is a continuum. At one extreme, there is full positive mental health, and at the other, there is mental illness or very poor mental health. Most people fluctuate somewhere between, experiencing full fitness and experiencing ill health throughout their lifetime. There are always some individuals who experience more chronic or severe poor health than others, be it mental or physical.

Mental health continuum

Mental health is influenced positively and negatively by a range of factors, such as the physical and social environment, poverty, relationships, stress and other health conditions.

Figure 1.1 Mental health as a continuum

Although there are definite links between poverty and poor mental health, mental illness can occur in any context and in any person. To promote positive mental health, it is important that school practitioners understand that everyone is somewhere on the mental health continuum and that mental health promotion is not the specialist role of health professionals. With that understanding, those who work to promote positive mental health can begin to recognise and, where possible, reduce or offset some of the social and environmental factors that influence mental health. Without this positive conception of mental health there is a danger that the 'stigma' of mental health will be reinforced.

Figure 1.2 Everyone has mental health

Components of positive mental health

Positive mental health is more than just the absence of mental illness. Definitions vary in the finer detail, but there is agreement that positive mental health has three components:

- the absence of persistent negative mood,
- the presence of positive mood,
- life satisfaction.

(Ryan and Deci, 2001; WHO, 1998)

So a child with positive mental health might not always be smiling and happy. They will get upset or angry or low at times, but they will also have times where they are happy, content and relaxed.

What is actually meant by 'life satisfaction' can vary between cultures, and the factors that influence life satisfaction can also be specific to a culture. When talking about children, life satisfaction usually relates to the child's self-esteem and self-concept. That is a child's feelings about their characteristics and qualities and their body image. Children are more likely to express or recognise satisfaction with life if they like themselves and the life they are experiencing. For example, there was a time in my daughter's life when life satisfaction was wholly dependent on the success of her beloved football team. This was actually because, in the rest of her life, she had few friends who had anything in common with her, and she did not enjoy anything at school, which she experienced as boring. Whereas now, she is satisfied with life as she likes who she is; she has good friends around her, and she is studying the things she enjoys.

Characteristics of positive mental health

Characteristics of positive mental health are the **ability** to:

- cope with crises,
- develop emotionally,
- experience enjoyment of life,
- feel optimism,
- feel a sense of achievement,
- experience life satisfaction,
- have a sense of fun.

The word **ability** is very important here. Positive mental health does not mean that someone is always happy or optimistic. Nor does it mean they are never sad or angry. Someone with positive mental health will experience the full range of emotions. It is only when a person gets stuck in a particular emotion, which might include a numb, almost emotionless state, that they might be experiencing or at risk of poor mental health.

Included within these characteristics of positive mental health are the ability to value self and having realistic confidence and self-esteem. Humphrey (2004) defines self-esteem as the evaluation of a person's self-concept compared to their ideal self. In the classroom this would be how a child sees themselves compared to the child they would like to be. It is important to emphasise and explain the word 'realistic' here. Realistic optimism is based on an accurate self-image in relation to the context. An unrealistic self-image is not necessarily healthy or desirable and can lead to misplaced or unfulfilled ambition or expectation. A child might have low self-esteem because they see themselves as slow and not as clever as their classmates. They only notice how quickly their friends finish a task, without actually realising that their slow, careful approach is giving them a good understanding and accuracy. Their ideal self is a fast worker rather than one who develops understanding. They can see the speed in others, but they cannot see the depth of understanding in themselves.

Obviously, there is far more to self-esteem than this, but this simple example is intended to illustrate how unrealistic views of the classroom can influence a child's self-esteem. As shall be explored in later chapters, there is much teachers can do to support their pupils to develop healthy, realistic self-esteem.

Excessively high self-esteem is associated with substance abuse and other risky behaviours. Unrealistic expectations or self-confidence, whether too high or too low, can damage life satisfaction. For example, consider the child who never dares to write because they believe they are not good enough or might get something wrong and the child who always picks the easy maths or PE challenge. These children may stay safe and never meet failure, but they will also not experience the satisfaction of overcoming barriers, trying something tricky and achieving success after effort.

At the other extreme, consider the overconfident child who gets into tricky situations because they think their skills are more advanced than they actually are. Consider also the child who has unrealistically high self-expectations that lead them to pick the hardest maths task or physical challenge every time, even though they end up in tears, unable to complete it.

In this way, positive mental health involves balance and proportion; rather than being about demonstrating only positive emotions and experiences, it includes a level of self-understanding and being able to reflect on self accurately, to build on past experiences and learn from them (Keyes, 2002). Self-awareness and life satisfaction are closely linked to the ability to cope with challenges.

Coping with challenges

Positive mental health allows individuals to cope with challenging or stressful experiences in addition to the normal stress of life (WHO, 1998). This coping is often known as resilience.

It is worth looking at several different definitions of resilience to get a clear understanding of what it actually means.

- Weare (2010:4) defines resilience as 'processing or bouncing back from difficult experiences'.
- Luthar, Cicchetti and Becker (2000:546) define it as 'the maintenance of positive adjustment under challenging life conditions'.
- Gu and Day (2013:40) state that it is 'the capacity to function well generally' rather than specifically in challenging times.

Discussion of resilience would fill a book in itself, but it is worth considering it in a little more detail in the context of the primary classroom. Taking Luthar, Cicchetti and Becker's definition, it would seem that if a child cannot carry on as normal in the face of challenge, then they do not have resilience. This would be an inaccurate interpretation. As Gu and Day's definition suggests, sometimes resilience is required to cope with life's general demands. Think about yourself. Are there times when you find even the routine chores at home, work or school almost too demanding? A great deal of emotional and mental energy can be consumed just functioning normally.

This takes me back to Weare's definition. Whether experiencing a routine challenge or extreme crisis, it is normal and healthy to have a reaction, to struggle a bit before bouncing back and coping. Tears, anger or sadness when experiencing a loss or difficulty are not evidence of a lack of resilience. They are likely to be part of a healthy coping mechanism, an aspect of resilience that actually helps the person bounce back. If we are promoting positive mental health, we should be exploring coping strategies, not expecting there to be none. I would be more concerned about the mental health of a child who experienced a loss but exhibited no sign of a reaction than of one whose behaviour and mood changed for a few days, weeks or months.

Resilience is a characteristic of positive mental health. However, resilience can both help a child maintain their positive mental health and be enhanced by a child's positive mental health. Resilience could come from being fully functioning, experiencing the full range of emotions, rather than repressing or denying any uncomfortable ones. Expressing anger or sorrow can be healthy, but disproportionate emotion, such as excessive persistent anger and the ensuing aggression or antisocial behaviour, is more likely to be an indicator of or contributor to poor mental health. Perhaps the art of resilience is knowing when to go on and when to take time out to recuperate. As teachers, we should be helping children find their own healthy coping strategies within a supportive environment, rather than projecting expectations on them.

Just like all the elements of positive mental health, resilience is influenced by external factors. It is enhanced by positive relationships and through experiencing positive emotions and emotional confidence. This is why the fostering of resilience is considered to be a key part of a school's promotion of positive mental health. Factors believed to promote individual resilience include good social skills, positive self-esteem and a sense of humour (Goroshit and Hen, 2016; Newman and Blackburn, 2002).

Those able to hold on to a sense of optimism and achievement or other similar characteristics of positive mental health are better able to look beyond the moment of crisis, to see meaning in it. As a result of this, they may be able to plan for the future, thus recovering from the crisis more rapidly or coping more effectively (Folkman and Moskowitz, 2000; Fredrickson and Joiner, 2002; Wright et al., 2010). In contrast, poor mental health can inhibit coping as it can cause a person to be less able to see a solution or to distract themselves, and thus they are less likely to seek support. Consider a child whose best friend moves to another school. If they believe that they will never be happy again, never have another friend and that they will lose all contact with their best friend, it makes the loss seem much more unbearable. They have no hope or belief that anything will ever be OK again. It is likely to take them a long time to be able to cope with the loss. Their resilience is low. But the loss will be experienced differently if, when their best friend moves away, they believe that they will make other good friends, that they will experience the same level of fun they have had with that friend with other friends and that they will see their best friend again. With this optimism, belief and hope, the loss will become easier to bear. The child will be more resilient.

Positive mental health is clearly more than an attitude or feeling, but emotions and emotional literacy are embedded within positive mental health. Positive emotions, such as enjoyment of life, optimism, a sense of achievement, satisfaction or fun, are crucial elements to staying mentally healthy. In this way, positive mental health is complex and multifaceted. Each element can enhance another in a reciprocal fashion. The opposite is also true: the absence of one element can erode another and so have a detrimental impact on mental health. We often talk about a child's emotional development or their social development, but, in actual fact, the two are so interrelated that it can be difficult to separate them out. Social and emotional wellbeing are fundamental elements of positive mental health.

As stated earlier, mental health is influenced by a range of factors. A key one of these is the social context. Positive and trusting relationships are essential to positive mental health. The teacher-pupil relationship is crucial to a child's positive experience in the classroom. There is evidence that those who are socially isolated can be at risk of poorer mental health. An individual influences the social context in which they live, work and study whilst also being influenced by the same social world. This makes the school's role in positive mental health promotion such a significant and relevant one.

This chapter presented:

- definitions of mental health as a continuum, something that everyone experiences;
- the main components of positive mental health;
- characteristics of positive mental health;
- discussion of the role of self-esteem, life satisfaction and self-confidence;
- resilience and coping.

It concludes that positive mental health is complex, multifaceted and influenced by many factors.

The chapter ends with the questions from the audit to evaluate staff knowledge and understanding of positive mental health.

Audit: questions for staff on teaching and understanding

The audit questions relating to school staff understanding of positive mental health are included here. Having read the chapter, are you now better able to answer them?

- Do you have a secure understanding of positive mental health? How would you define it?
- What might a child with positive mental health be like?
- What might a child with poor mental health be like?
- Do you teach children about emotional health or mental health?
- What kinds of things do you do?
- What explicit teaching do you do related to fostering the many elements of positive mental health promotion?
- What embedded practice do you have in place to promote positive mental health?

2 Positive mental health promotion in schools

This chapter looks at the basis for promoting positive mental health in primary schools and at the importance of the teacher to a child's wellbeing and ability to thrive. There is consideration of the asset and deficit models of promotion, drawing from research in schools. The connections between good primary practice and positive mental health promotion are discussed, and, without prioritising academic achievement, the academic basis for positive mental health promotion is presented.

Defining positive mental health promotion

Positive mental health promotion is defined as any effort taken to increase the social and emotional wellbeing of a group, society or individuals (WHO, 1998). Promotion includes actions designed to increase both an individual's and a community's capacity to experience and maintain positive mental health. (Adelman and Taylor, 2010; National Institute for Health and Clinical Excellence (NICE), 2008; WHO, 1998). In school, this means implementing an approach or range of approaches that help individual children to develop positive mental health whilst making sure that these approaches also contribute to the positive mental health of all the children in the class and school community.

The World Health Organisation (1998) places emphasis on promotion as the 'process of enabling people to increase control over, and to improve, their health' (WHO, 1998:3). Promotion is about empowerment, which requires action to build the knowledge, skills and attitudes necessary for social and emotional development and a mentally healthy life. In the past there has been quite a strong focus in education on helping children develop knowledge about health and what is healthy or dangerous. However, as the WHO definition and Adelman and Taylor's (2006) advice make clear, promotion is much more than developing a healthy knowledge base. Empowerment requires the development of skills, attitudes and even characteristics so that, as well as knowing what positive mental health means, children also have the ability and experience to be mentally healthy.

These definitions begin to make clear that positive mental health promotion in schools is not just about taught lessons and subject knowledge. It is about the provision of a health promoting ethos, one which, according to Herrman, Saxena and Moodie (2005), respects and protects the rights of the individual.

In this way, positive mental health promotion is about individuals and environments. Reviews of positive mental health promotion literature conclude that, to be effective, promotion has to operate on three levels:

1 empowering individuals,
2 strengthening communities and environment so that they are supportive and nurturing,
3 reducing barriers to positive mental health and its promotion.

Two contrasting approaches to positive mental health promotion

There are two dominant models of positive mental health promotion:

- asset, also referred to as a wellness or universal model,
- deficit.

The asset model recognises that mental health is a continuum rather than an illness. It takes a holistic approach to promoting positive mental health for all.

The deficit model works on the basis that removing mental illness will result in positive mental health. It sets out to remove and reduce risks to mental health.

If we return briefly to the Chapter 1 definitions, we can see that the predominant view of positive mental health is that of a continuum along which most people's mental health fluctuates throughout a lifetime. The WHO (2001) clearly and repeatedly state that mental health is more than the absence of mental illness. Current policy in Scotland and across much of the world also recognises positive mental health as a continuum. In such countries, consistent with this definition, the positive mental health promotion guidance and policy draws on the asset or wellness model and sets out to promote positive mental health holistically and for all.

Promotion through a deficit model used to be more prevalent in education and society generally. Health-promoting actions often set out merely to remove risks to health: for example, through educating children on the dangers of substance abuse or advising them to tell someone if they were being bullied. There was often a far greater focus on physical health because the risks to this were much more tangible and recognisable. While raising awareness of risks to health is an important part of health promotion, it is not health promotion. If we want children and adults to make healthy choices, they have to learn about more than the risks. They will need to develop, understand and apply healthy attitudes, characteristics, skills and knowledge within a health-promoting environment.

To illustrate this in the context of the classroom, I will return to the reference to bullying. If as teachers, we recognise that bullying is a risk to health and seek to reduce it, is it sufficient merely to tell children what to do if they are bullied? Does this mean that the adults then step in and stop the bullies? How would this be empowering the children to live healthily? Quite clearly, such action alone is not sufficient and will not contribute to enabling children 'to increase control over, and to improve, their health' (WHO, 1998:3). In order to reduce bullying and increase a child's ability to stay well in the face of such behaviour, we need to return to the idea of promotion as being about individuals, community and environment. A more effective promotion approach aimed at reducing bullying will look at all the children, bullied, bullies and bystanders, and at the classroom or school environment. It will seek to build healthy social and emotional capacities and characteristics in the children, working to address the factors that cause children both to bully and to be vulnerable to bullying. Alongside this, there should be work to provide a respecting, nurturing and safe environment. There are many other factors to be taken into consideration, not least of which is a good knowledge of the children, issues and context so that approaches are appropriate to the needs of the children and classroom.

As you can see, a holistic asset approach is complex and multifaceted. It is much more than removal of risks or teaching on how to avoid a risk. The deficit model used on its own can lead to the seemingly random, unsustainable and inconsistent application of prevention strategies. However, this does not mean that there is no place for strategies targeted at removing specific risk to health or those targeted at a small group of 'at-risk' children. What is sometimes called a multicomponent approach to positive mental health promotion involves the creation of a supportive environment, the strengthening of community and the development of personal skills whilst also aiming to reduce or remove causes of poor mental health. Research into most effective promotion suggests that school positive mental health promotion is most effective if it combines such an asset approach for all with targeted interventions that reduce specific risk factors or support the mental health of an identified groups of children.

The teacher's role in positive mental health promotion

Primary school teachers spend so much time with their classes that they play a significant role in a child's life. So much so that whether or not a child likes school tends to depend on the relationship that they have with their teacher. A positive classroom environment makes it more possible to build these close, supportive and trusting relationships between teacher and pupil. However, the relationships in turn shape the environment. The child's whole experience of school can be defined by the caring interactions between the teacher and the child. Murray and Pianta (2007) argue that teachers are actually in a *unique position* to make a significant contribution to positive mental health promotion. It is not only teachers who are aware of the importance of their relationships with pupils. Older children often also recognise that their behaviour and way of relating to others in the class is influenced by their relationship with the teacher.

Good quality teacher-pupil relationships are beneficial to a child's academic achievement and engagement with school and to their healthy social and emotional development. The support teachers give through these relationships provides a protective factor for child wellbeing. These positive relationships also foster resilience. A child is better able to cope in challenging times if they have a positive relationship with their teacher and friends. Characteristics of such a beneficial relationship include warmth, trust, openness, consistency, support and teaching. Teachers have a pivotal role in positive mental health promotion, but they do need to be part of a wider system. One person alone cannot promote positive mental health.

Rationale for promoting positive mental health in schools

As positive mental health promotion is so connected to environment and community, it becomes more apparent that if we wish to promote the mental health of children and young people, then the school community in which they spend so much of their time has to be an active participant in promotion.

In their studies of mental health promotion, Adelman and Taylor (2010) conclude that any attempt to improve the mental health of society must involve schools. Mental health promotion is a community responsibility rather than that of each individual. Collectively, everyone in the school has a responsibility to contribute to the promotion of their own and other community members' positive mental health. The flip side is that everyone in the school is also capable of having a detrimental impact on the health of the community.

We know that lifelong patterns of behaviour and relationships are established during childhood. Positive mental health promotion in childhood can increase self-worth, reducing the risk of mental health problems in later life. Schools are important social contexts. They are the main place in which children develop relationships with adults and other children (Hornby and Atkinson, 2003; Zins et al., 2004) and make the most significant contribution to a child's social development. Children need to feel emotionally safe in school, which can be achieved through well-planned and consistent policies of pastoral care and positive mental health promotion. Support from teachers, clear rules, a well-organised routine and a positive behaviour policy contribute to a school environment in which pupils feel safe and a sense of belonging (Lynn, McKay and Atkins, 2003; Murray and Pianta, 2007).

If we review the research literature in this way, it becomes clear that to engage fully in academic life and to get the most benefit from their time in school, children need to develop social and emotional competences within an environment that provides positive role models and opportunities for the children to practice their skills. Primary schools generally already have strong pastoral care systems, and most teachers are aware of the importance of caring, supportive classroom environments and positive relationships. With this in mind, it would seem that schools and teachers are already experienced in and committed to social and emotional wellbeing promotion. Is it the term 'positive mental health' that leads some teachers to profess a lack of confidence in this area? One of the aims of this book is to help school practitioners see the links between what teachers already do well and positive mental health promotion so that, when working to increase promotion, teachers are aware that they are usually starting from a position of knowledge and experience. Positive mental health promotion is not solely the domain of mental health practitioners. Teachers are specialists and can be the experts in positive classroom mental health promotion.

Whether actively engaged in promotion or otherwise, schools have a significant impact, positive or negative, on pupils' mental health, supporting the argument that mental health promotion is a school responsibility. However, schools are placed under increasingly strong pressure to evidence their effectiveness, and, rather than child wellbeing, pupil attainment is often seen as the measure for this. Such emphasis on accountability does not address the social, emotional and mental barriers to learning. It can sometimes be hard for an individual teacher or school leader to justify a focus on any kind of wellbeing promotion to policy makers, inspectors and sometimes even parents. There can be a tension between the pressure for attainment and the responsibility or desire to promote positive mental health. Teachers might find it easier to justify promotion more as part of their role if they could explain how positive mental health can reduce barriers to learning and increase pupils' ability to achieve their academic potential.

So it is important to look at the evidence and get a case together to show how focusing on positive mental health promotion supports academic attainment rather than taking time or resources away.

The relationship between positive mental health and learning

For over 20 years, the World Health Organisation (1998) has been advising that for children to engage fully with education they need to be emotionally healthy. Emotional and mental health problems are barriers to learning. Cushman, Clelland and Hornby (2011) are not alone in their claims that emotional wellbeing and academic success are 'interrelated and mutually supported' (248) and that mentally healthy children with positive self-esteem and social competence are better learners. Zins et al. (2004) claim that an integrated approach to wellbeing promotion can also improve children's academic achievements. Although not intended as their primary goal, many programmes designed to promote positive social and emotional or mental wellbeing also have a positive impact on learning.

Wide-scale evaluation and review in the USA of programmes to increase social and emotional learning found overwhelming evidence that the programmes had a positive impact on learning. In addition to experiencing social and emotional benefits, children also had improved numeracy and literacy skills (Greenberg et al., 2003; Zins et al., 2004). Other outcomes of social and emotional mental health promotion interventions and strategies evaluated include greater connectedness to school, reduced disruptive or antisocial behaviour and increased pro-social behaviour, higher self-esteem, higher self-belief and self- expectation, less hopelessness and increased emotional literacy. All of these can have a direct impact on learning and the positive learning environment of the classroom. When pupils received higher levels of support from teachers, this resulted in a reduction in distress and increased academic achievement and attainment (Lynn, McKay and Atkins, 2003).

When wellbeing and attainment are combined as aims of education, school becomes a more enjoyable place to learn. Rothman and McMillan's (2003) research into school ethos in Australia found a correlation between positive school climate where children felt a sense of belonging to their school and higher scores in maths and literacy.

The empowerment that comes from mentally healthy characteristics such as a sense of achievement, realistic self-efficacy and the confidence to succeed leads to greater motivation. Such motivation is positively associated with academic success. It prompts children to find out more and engage more in their studies, making them more likely to engage in their work willingly. Such positive mental health and empowerment increases independence and academic resilience. This allows children to persevere at a tricky task and then experience the heightened sense of achievement from such a challenge.

Effective practice

In summary, the most effective positive mental health promotion in schools requires:

- a planned approach incorporating long-term strategies,
- whole-school policies,
- actions and strategies to increase health-promoting elements and reduce factors likely to reduce wellbeing,
- a combination of universal approaches for all and targeted approaches for some,
- pupil involvement in the planning and understanding of the approaches,
- good collaboration between school staff,
- support for staff wellbeing,
- ownership by all within the school,
- partnership with parents,
- effective communication and collaboration with other health promotion agencies,
- approaches that are compatible with the local community,
- a planned approach informed by the needs of the school community,
- strong inspirational leadership invested in mental health promotion.

The following chapters in this book go into detail on the practicalities and specifics of elements of positive mental health promotion. This chapter concludes with a brief comparison between mental health-promoting elements and elements of good teaching or good schools.

Good teaching and positive mental health promotion

Research into what makes a good teacher tends to highlight the importance of relationships and personal characteristics such as enthusiasm, passion, commitment, dedication, humour, concern and ability to inspire (Benekos, 2016). Commitment, passion and enjoyment also feature highly in teachers' attitudes towards their role as promoters of positive mental health, which by Benekos' (2016) criteria would make them not only effective at positive mental health promotion but also better teachers. Benekos (2016) argues that personal attributes rather than pedagogical skill are what characterise a good teacher. One of the most significant ways in which teachers can promote positive mental health is through drawing on their personal qualities, the qualities that make them good teachers. Positive mental health promotion requires practice that is nonjudgemental, where teachers value each child in their class, listen carefully to the children's feelings and problems and respond empathically and sensitively. In this way, teachers meet a clearly identified need. Being listened to and heard in this way featured highly in Scottish young people's discussion of what influenced their positive mental health (Elsley and McMellon, 2010). Teachers who create such an ethos of care in their classroom build strong, positive relationships with their pupils whilst facilitating positive friendships between pupils. In this way, good teachers already have the skills and qualities fundamental to positive mental health promotion.

Characteristics of a good teacher include strong:

- professional knowledge;
- pedagogical skills;

- positive relationships;
- personal values;
- creation of a safe, trusting, stimulating and respecting environment;
- intellectual and emotional commitment;
- personal characteristics such as enthusiasm, passion, humour, concern and ability to inspire;
- ability to make context specific decisions and use judgement or the wisdom of practice;
- emotional literacy;
- integrity.

Positive mental health promotion requires:

- positive relationships;
- a supportive ethos;
- care and personal investment in teaching and the children;
- a focus on the whole child, not just the academic learner;
- planned delivery of skills or capacity-building teaching;
- classroom codes consistent with positive mental health promotion;
- a teacher embodying positive mental health (and a school that supports staff wellbeing);
- opportunities for the child to achieve, face challenges and experience success;
- opportunities for both teachers and children to enjoy being in the classroom.

There is a great deal of overlap between these two lists. The language may change, but the substance is similar. It does depend on a teacher's individual concept of what it is to be a teacher, but the majority of teachers, including all those in my recent research, could not identify anything in the list of positive mental health promotion requirements that they saw as incompatible with their role as teachers or outside their confidence or knowledge base. Sadly, one of the hardest to achieve was often enjoyment for all, but perhaps, with a coordinated, well planned whole-school strategy for positive mental health promotion in which staff are supported and valued, some beneficial enjoyment will be easier to find!

In this chapter, positive mental health promotion was defined as action taken to improve the mental health of an individual, group, community or society.

Two traditions of promotion were identified: asset, a holistic approach, and deficit, which seeks to remove risks to positive mental health.

The role of school and the importance of teachers was explored.

The benefits of promotion to learning and attainment were identified.

Positive mental health promotion was compared with the characteristics of good teaching.

Part II

How to promote positive mental health

Introduction to part II

Positive mental health promotion in a primary school requires the creation of a positive, supportive ethos in which both the children and the teacher feel valued, respected, included and safe. Positive relationships are fundamental to this ethos and, in turn, are enhanced or eroded by the ethos. Positive relationships and ethos are, in turn, influenced by the emotional literacy of those within the classroom. It may be necessary to take targeted action to improve specific relationship or social skills or to develop pupil and teacher emotional literacy in order to achieve the desired nurturing and health-promoting ethos. As part of ethos creation, the teacher needs to model and set expectations that exemplify and match the positive relationships and emotional literacy desirable to positive mental health promotion.

It becomes clear that, although we can separate artificially the elements of positive mental health promotion, they are, in fact, interlinked and overlapping as figure 12.1 attempts to demonstrate.

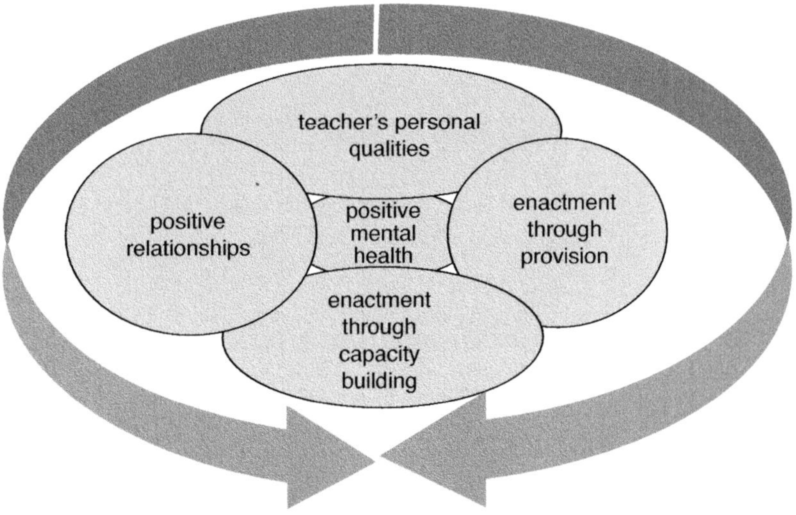

Figure 12.1 Interlinked relationship

Part Two of this book looks at the elements in turn for easy reference, but as you begin to embed or develop positive mental health promotion in your context, you will need to consider all or many of the elements simultaneously. So where do you start? Effective positive mental health promotion, as discussed in Chapter Two, is specific to context. Therefore, the best place to start is with an honest and multifaceted scrutiny of the current situation. Sample audit documents can be found in the Appendix. Questions for consideration are included in each chapter.

3 Positive relationships

This chapter discusses the fundamental importance of the teacher's relationship with the children. It builds on the skills and qualities of teachers discussed in Chapter 2 and explains how these can be used to promote positive relationships. It includes practical examples of ways in which social and emotional skills and attitudes can be nurtured so that the children are able to benefit from positive relationships with each other and the teacher.

The importance of positive relationships

As the literature discussed in Chapters 1 and 2 makes clear, the friendships a child has in school and the relationship they have with the teacher shape the quality of the child's whole school experience. The social environment and these relationships are fundamental to a child's mental health because, in primary schools, the class teacher is a significant person in the child's life. Children spend so much time in school that the friendships and relationships with other children have the power to support or demote each child's positive mental health.

However, supporting positive relationships in the classroom is not a new act or additional task for the busy teacher to carry out in order to promote positive mental health. It happens already. Whether doing so to promote positive mental health or to get the behaviour environment right, primary school teachers embed strategies to promote a positive social environment into their daily routines:

> Getting to know them, you discover what matters. It was just for some children, that little thing, that cloud that has been overhanging them for goodness knows how long, it's just been something lifted and they can be a different person; just for that one thing. That's why teaching is so difficult because you have 30 children in front of you who all have clouds over their heads.
>
> (Primary School Teacher)

The aim here is to make clear the connection between positive relationships and positive mental health promotion, as indicated in the words of the teacher quoted here. In my research, all the teachers involved cited positive relationships as one of the most important elements of their role as a teacher and the work they did to promote wellbeing. What is interesting, but probably to be expected, is that there is great diversity in what is actually meant by positive relationships. Before exploring ways in which to build and promote positive relationships, this chapter will first consider varying interpretations of the term.

Consistent with research into motivation to teach and concepts of teaching, the nature of a positive relationship between teacher and pupils is shaped by how we see ourselves as teachers and what we see as the purpose of teaching.

Concepts of teaching - motivation to teach

Questions to consider

Why do you teach?
Are you here primarily to ensure that children can read, write, do maths, understand history, speak French, learn science and geography?
What is your pastoral responsibility to the children?
Why are the children at school?
Do you see the child as just a learner or do you recognise the whole child?
How do you see your relationship with the pupils?
How do you want them to see you or relate to you?

This next section takes two extreme perspectives of teaching and positive relationships, with the acknowledgement that most teachers are likely to be more of a mixture:

a) Teachers who see themselves as authority figures, there to impart knowledge and help the children get the best academic attainment, have a concept of positive relationships that focuses on academic learning or attainment.
b) Teachers who see themselves as there to nurture the whole child, to help individuals achieve their potential are more likely to have a more holistic concept of the teacher-pupil relationship.

a) In an academic attainment-focused perspective on building positive relationships with pupils, the teacher might:

- let the children know the teacher is in charge,
- find out about the children from their previous teacher,
- make expectations clear,
- let the children know the consequences of the choices they make,
- tell the children how to behave/relate to each other and the teacher,
- read the pupil record to find out about the child,
- explain the class rules,
- read any notes about the parents and child's background to get to know them better.

b) In a holistic perspective on building positive relationships with pupils, the teacher might:

- share appropriate personal facts to let the children see the teacher as a human;
- show interest in the children and their lives;
- have fun with the children;
- model and articulate emotions;
- be honest and open, having the humility to admit when they get something wrong;
- show respect;
- have clear expectations and help children identify the potential consequences of their choices;
- be consistent and reliable, firm but fair;
- know, value and care about the whole child;
- listen;
- build positive relationships with parents;
- be approachable;
- be trustworthy;
- facilitate class negotiation of the rules;
- be a role model for positive relationships.

To reiterate, these are polarised extremes, and most teachers will draw from both, but the artificial separation in this way helps to illustrate the importance of working out what positive relationships mean to you in your classroom and finding out whether this is consistent with the whole-school perspective.

Strategies and approaches to fostering positive relationships within the classroom

Figure 3.1 shows the ways in which the ability to engage in positive relationships is contingent on many layers and factors. Chapter 5 explores the role of emotional literacy in more detail.

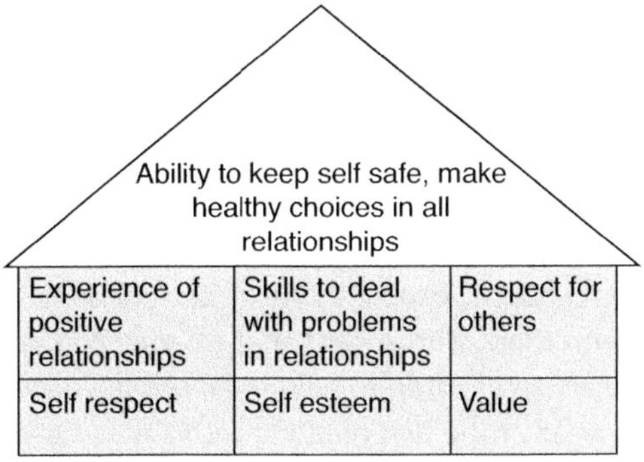

Figure 3.1 Relationships

If, as a teacher, you are having difficulty building and maintaining positive relationships between yourself and the pupils or between pupils, it may be necessary to go back and see whether some of the personal attitudes, capacities and skills important to positive relationships need to be targeted specifically for development. Sometimes it is not the way we seek to build relationships that is wrong; it is that the children do not have the necessary skills. This is why teaching is so difficult. Every child is different. Every class is different, and the same teacher will have to find different ways to connect to and establish a rapport with individual children in different ways each year as shall be discussed later in this chapter.

Starting with the teacher

There is no teacher who does not start the school year thinking about the new class and how they will get to know them. This core element of positive mental health promotion does not demand specialist skills or knowledge. The building, strengthening and promoting of positive relationships within a classroom is part of the teacher's role whilst also being fundamental to healthy social, emotional and mental development.

This being the case, as a teacher, you will already have your own experiences and approaches to building relationships. There is certainly a wealth of schemes, strategies and books already in existence that support this element of the primary school teacher's role. The intention in this chapter is to review those approaches through the lens of positive mental health promotion: positive relationships as a way to promote positive mental health.

The key elements in the teacher's role in developing and maintaining positive relationships with their pupils are:

- being human;
- working with the whole child, not just concerned with study;
- positive regard;
- capacity building:
  - knowing or finding out what strengths the children have for their relationships;
  - finding out specific areas for development that need to be addressed in individuals and the whole class so that they are able to engage in positive relationships.

Being human

We do not know what perceptions, expectations or assumptions about their teacher each child brings into school with them. This means that we may need to emphasise a particular aspect of ourselves with certain children to help them see beyond a false perception. But at the very beginning of the year or the first meeting with a new class, it is important to let the children meet the human being as well as the teacher figure.

Ways to do this will depend on who you are, the school context and the children in the school. One successful approach is to bring in 'my special box' and to share the contents with the children gradually over the first few days or weeks, whilst also giving them time to gather their own box (or list of things to bring in from home). There is of course the need to maintain professional boundaries, but the purpose of the box is to help the children see you as a human being as well as a teacher.

Your personal box might include:

Contents of a Special Box	*Specific Examples*
A souvenir from a favourite holiday	Tent pegs - I love camping
A photo	Me with my first class
Something related to a hobby	Cycling gloves or cycle map
	A packet of seeds
	My favourite book
A letter or card from a pupil	A goodbye gift from a pupil
	A thank-you card from a parent
Graduation photograph	Graduation photo
Newspaper cutting	A newspaper article with a photo of me and some former pupils celebrating when we saved the school from closure
Something related to a struggle or challenge	Son's hospital bracelet from when he was rushed to hospital as a baby

This can be a token gesture that falls flat, or it can be a genuine way to get the children to engage with you. It all depends on how genuine you are with your explanation of each treasure you share. The contents are not as important as the glimpse of the person that the children meet when each item is revealed. Put in things that are important to you but which you are happy to share. You will need to gauge the tone and receptivity of the class to determine which you reveal and when. Some classes will need you to work slowly through and share the contents over several weeks to give you time to sort out any other immediate concerns in the classroom. It is sensible to gauge the children's response to vulnerability before introducing the item related to a struggle or challenge.

The children get to see something important to you as a person, particularly within the professional sphere through the school-related items. But, more importantly, as you reveal each item, you have the opportunity to demonstrate the emotion associated with the item. In this way you are both strengthening and modelling positive relationships, as well as modelling emotional literacy.

I will now take some of the examples above to illustrate the opportunities for the children to see the emotional and human characteristics of their teacher:

- Tent pegs: the children get to hear their teacher talking passionately about something they love. They do not just learn that Ms Holt goes camping, but they meet the enthusiast. They see what she looks like and how she sounds when she is excited and enthusiastic about something.
- Thank-you card from a parent: the children are reminded that teachers and parents have a relationship - they talk to each other and work together sometimes for the child. With a bit of background information, the children also get to hear how surprised/touched/embarrassed their teacher was to receive a thank-you card from this parent.

Once early relationships are established, some of the more tricky special items can be shared.

- The newspaper article about saving the school provides opportunities to talk with anger or indignation that the council tried to close the school, to talk with pride about the way the parents, teachers, pupils and whole village pulled together to save the school from closure. The children see a range of emotions and may be able to identify with them or be aware of how they might have felt under the circumstances.
- Finally, the hospital identity bracelet provides the opportunity to see the teacher as a parent and one who was worried about her child. It raises opportunities for the children to share their own experiences of hospitals and illness.

From these examples, it should become clear that it is not so much the content of the box but the genuine way in which the importance of each item is shared with the children, allowing the teacher to show a variety of emotions. Each item shared in this way also provides opportunities for the children to respond emotionally, drawing on their whole life experience, not just as learners.

After experiencing a tutor modelling her own special box to demonstrate how to do this with children, a teaching student admitted:

> I thought it was going to be a corny activity, but the emotion in her voice as she shared some of those things with me made me see her in a whole new way. They really meant something to her. Respect to Clara for being so real.

Teachers who uses this approach with their classes explained the benefits:

> The children enjoy what the teacher shares, and it gives them an idea of life experiences that maybe they're not going to be doing yet, like buying houses. It's good for them to hear how you're doing that, the processes involved, how you felt and the skills you needed for that experience. The children genuinely want to know about our lives.
>
> I was glad I shared the hospital story with my class because I think the children genuinely felt so important to be given that information. They are important to me, but that made them feel important. It's crucial that they do feel appreciated and valued and not always in adversity.

If, over the first few weeks, the children are given time and support to develop their own special boxes, they, too, will have the opportunity to share chosen elements of their lives with the teacher and their classmates. They get to know each other and the teacher, whilst the teacher is also able to get a better understanding of the whole child. The next chapter explores the importance of ethos to positive mental health promotion, but it is important to note here that these emerging positive relationships will be enhanced by a nurturing environment. By introducing many different facets of the teacher and child as human beings, there is a level of trust. Alongside the relationship building, the need for positive regard and respectful treatment and response to the feelings and offerings of others is essential. As the environment can promote wellbeing and positive relationships, it can also demote them if we get it wrong.

There will be a range of other beginning-of-the-year actions and processes going on in the classroom to help the teacher and pupils get to know each other within the context of lessons and classroom routines. There are also many more ways in which to establish relationships, but with mental health promotion as the priority, it is as much about how the relationship building takes place as what is actually done. The next section continues the theme of teacher-pupil relationships with a consideration of the core characteristics essential to health-promoting relationships.

Teacher-pupil relationships - whole child, not just study

As the teacher introduces the child to various aspects of themselves beyond that of teacher, the teacher also needs to get to know the whole child. Positive mental health promotion works best when it is holistic and working to nurture the whole child, not just focusing on supporting the child as a learner.

The nature of the children in the class - the mix and the individual characters - will determine how easy or challenging it is to establish positive relationships with them. Being realistic, it can take a long time with some classes: for example, those with children who have not been together as a whole class before, with those who have had a tricky experience the previous year as a class (perhaps a succession of supply teachers) or with those classes that contain a significant number of vulnerable or hurt children. These classes that are hard to connect to are usually those who need the most support and who will benefit most from positive mental health promotion and positive relationships with each other and their teacher.

It can take time and it can be difficult to establish positive relationships, even when the class teacher is doing all the 'right things'. It is important not to give up. Whilst being reflective and reviewing the appropriateness of approaches taken, it is essential that teachers give the approaches and strategies they are using time to work and that they do not introduce a succession of short-term initiatives or approaches. Yes, if something really is not working, it should be changed, but frequent changes increase the feelings of instability the children may be experiencing. There will be a sense of inconsistency and a reluctance for the children to engage in things that may not be around next week.

However long it might take, the teacher needs to prioritise getting to know the whole child, not just the one they see in the classroom but the child inside and outside school, their strengths and abilities. Every child is different socially and emotionally, as well as academically. To foster positive relationships and promote positive mental health, teachers need to find out where a child is emotionally and what they need, aware that they will not all be in the same place or capable of the same level of social and emotional engagement.

Once a teacher knows the children in their class well, they can use this knowledge as a way to gauge, monitor and support the wellbeing of the children in their class:

> Knowing your children, you can see straightaway in the morning if something's not right with a child. And it's then having the time to say 'What's happened? What's made you feel that way?'

It is becoming increasingly common to build in some check-in time when the children arrive in the morning. As the teacher greets each child, the child feels valued and welcome when they come into school. Some schools plan set times for these catch-ups or check-ins first thing in the morning, and others have systems in place so that teachers and children can note when a check-in is needed and follow this up at some point during the day.

It helps children to know that when they come into school, they will have the opportunity to show whether they have any concerns, problems or joys. This can be done through emotions boards where the child uses a symbol to indicate their feelings or needs. Worry boxes can be a more discreet way of voicing a concern. For younger children, having a teddy or class character they can share their news with or give their name card to can be another way for the child to demonstrate that they have something to share and for them to know that their feelings matter.

After the initial relationship-building phase, there is a need for consistency and maintenance of the same values and social behaviours in the ongoing relationships. Positive relationships have to be worked on continuously. Honesty, consistency and nurture all feature prominently in descriptions of positive relationships as these comments from teachers demonstrate:

> The children will value you more for it if you are honest with them.
>
> You have to be absolutely frank with them. We're not afraid to tell them when they are getting it wrong, and they are resilient for that. They are not getting false praise, and they know that they are not getting away with things.
>
> Being that consistent, trustworthy person who is interested in them as people is paramount.

One of the difficulties for teachers can be how they maintain the positive relationships whilst also making sure the ethos is productive and behaviour is not impeding learning. How do we continue to show positive regard when needing to reinforce a class code?

Positive regard

Positive regard is defined as offering an attitude of acceptance and non-judgementalism. (Rogers, 1980). It is deemed an essential component of a relationship that supports healthy growth and development. In education, this means accepting and valuing the child, even if their behaviour or language is not necessarily acceptable. This makes it easier for the teacher to see the potential in every child and not write off a child because of their circumstances or the way they relate to others. When teachers look at each child, they need to make sure that they see the child and that what they see is not misshapen by assumptions, generalisations or background knowledge, as summed up by this teacher:

> Just trying not to label children, not to look at them and see the families or the last test they did or what it says about their attainment in my folder, but remembering that they all have the capacity to learn, they all have the capacity to change and grow and develop and that pigeonholing is not helpful.

There is a fine line between creating a bond with pupils and maintaining authority. In teaching we are used to separating behaviour from the child, but this is actually also an essential part of developing and maintaining a positive relationship with pupils. There will always be times when a teacher has to make clear to a child that their behaviour is not acceptable. No matter how positive our relationships and how much we use positive reinforcement to maintain the productive learning environment, there will still be times when we have to reprimand a child - tell them not to do something or that they have done something inappropriate. Although we may be separating the behaviour from the child, the child does not necessarily know that. It helps to maintain the relationships if, after having to reprimand a child, we can come back to them within a short while and praise them for something they are doing right or admire something they have done or are doing, as this quote illustrates:

> If I do have to speak to a child quite sternly, I make sure I get back to them before lunchtime or the end of the day with just something like, 'I like that coat you are wearing', something short and snappy so the child knows it's past that awkward stage.

It helps everyone when, within an established relationship, the children know where they stand with their teacher and what to expect.

> They can enjoy themselves and learn and be confident, but they know that if they cross boundaries, I'll pull them up for it. One of mine has written in her jotter, 'Miss B is very funny and we have a good time with her, but she's strict when she has to be'.

It is important for teachers to take an emotional step back and not take behaviours personally. Instead, they should try to figure out what was behind a child's behaviour. These quotes from health promoting primary teachers give some insight into how they do this:

> It's recognising you've got to tell them off, but it's the digging deeper into why that happened. Thinking 'What's going on in your head?' and recognising that there is more to it. It is coming across as the authoritative figure but also as a caring figure. I am here to help you as well.
>
> I have been looking at children's emotions and how they display their emotions and what their behaviour is telling me rather than just seeing it as behaviour . . . Making sure I get to know them as a person and give that message that I can still value you as a person even when you are behaving in this way.

In this way, children should know that it is not the end of the world, that they will not be disliked if they have their behaviour reprimanded or if they are struggling with their work in the classroom. The teacher is not labelling a child for their actions nor are they demonising a child. Instead, they are isolating the behaviour and continuing to show the child positive regard:

> We don't demonise anyone; we acknowledge that everyone gets angry. We don't tell children off for emotional responses, but we contextualise it for them, talk it through with them.

We are all human beings, and such continuous positive regard can be hard sometimes, particularly if, as teachers, we have invested a great deal of thought, time, emotional energy and care into something, and it does not go down well or is rejected by a child or the class. It is hard to maintain that fair and consistent approach and positive regard when we are feeling hurt. It is important that we find healthy ways to manage this. There is more discussion of this in Chapter 9, where teacher wellbeing is discussed.

Consistent with the positive regard towards each child and the separation of the child from their actions is the need for a clean slate. Nothing is more demotivating for a child than to lose their chance of a positive response or reward on a Monday morning and know that it has now gone for the rest of the week. The practice of 'golden time' is a common one. Children spend the week earning the entitlement to some free choice or fun activity on a Friday. The rationale is one of positive reinforcement, reward rather than sanction. However, it does not work if there is no way to recover from a transgression. If a child loses golden time on Monday, what is the point of behaving well or working hard or being a good citizen for the rest of the week, particularly if they have to put a great deal of effort into doing and being those things?

A clean slate policy, however, gives everyone the chance of starting fresh. Rewards should be short term or redeemable. With a clean slate policy, a child comes into school every day knowing that they have a fresh start, that the transgressions or struggles of the previous day will be set aside, and they will be able to shine. They can come into school with more enthusiasm and motivation - happier - which then makes positive interactions and academic achievement much more possible. This does not mean that any behaviour goes, and chaos reigns in the classroom. That would not be health promoting for anyone! Rather, it means that issues are dealt with quickly, and the child is aware that it is the behaviour that is at issue rather than the child. This allows them to maintain a level of realistic self-esteem and optimism essential for positive mental health.

Similarly, with a clean slate, the teacher does not write off a child and starts each day open to the possibility of success and positive relationships. They do not hold a child's behaviour against them. This avoids the downward spiral where a teacher expects a child to behave poorly and so relates to them in such a way that the child then behaves according to expectations because anything else is not recognised. The child's wellbeing deteriorates, and so does their behaviour and ability to engage in positive relationships.

When you get it right, human connection between teacher and pupil allows teachers to be positive role models for relationships. The benefits to this are multiple, but one raised by the majority of participants in my recent study (Holt, 2019) was that the connection to the teacher and peers meant that many children who had done something outside the behaviour code barely needed to be told off as they were disappointed in themselves for letting down the teacher with whom they had the trusting relationship:

> They are disappointed and worried about letting you down because of that relationship. They want you to be proud of them. They don't want you to be upset.

This promotes everyone's wellbeing because a classroom that feels like a good place to be and work is much more healthy than a classroom full of reprimands and disagreements.

If, as teachers, we want to build and maintain positive relationships with the children in our class as a way to promote positive mental health, we need to know each child, to listen and be open to change.

Pupil-pupil relationships - capacity building

Helping the children develop positive relationships with each other is, again, supported by the reinforcement of the requisite social skills and emotional literacy within the classroom and environment (as explored further in Chapter 4). Teaching of specific strategies or social skills helps children form positive relationships. However, if the development of interpersonal skills is restricted to work in specific lessons, these can often be overlooked or not valued. The emphasis needs to be on embedding good practice into the daily life of the classroom and on the importance of the teacher as a role model in doing this. The children and teacher have to be able to apply the skills gained across their lives and not just within the set lessons. This is easier to achieve if the opportunities and connections are made explicit wherever they occur so children can see the relevance of the social skills they have been exploring to both their time in school and their life outside the school. See Chapter 7 and Appendix 20 for ways to do this.

Teachers already know the importance of social skills and peer relationships in the classroom and work to develop and support these. In this way, teachers are already well placed to promote positive mental health in their pupils. The focus in this next section is on highlighting key elements and their relevance to positive mental health.

Healthy social and emotional development are characteristics of positive mental health. It sounds obvious to state that social skills cannot be developed in isolation, but it can leave one wondering where to start - with the social skills or the relationships? Engaging in positive relationships can help a child's health and social and emotional development whilst, in turn, healthy social and emotional development is required in order to engage fully in positive relationships. Every child will be different and have their own social and emotional development needs. Differentiation is needed here just as in any taught area of the school curriculum.

Sometimes it is obvious when a child has difficulty engaging in friendships. The most effective way to support them with this is only determined by knowing the child well and understanding why they are having difficulty. Sometimes, the reasons are complex and mean that the child actually has significantly poor mental health and perhaps needs the intervention of specialists. Unless specialists are already involved, it is always worth starting with the relevant skills development or opportunity creation and then seeking advice from professionals if the social and emotional difficulties persist. Whilst supporting children with consistently poor mental health is more specialist, any work that supports that child will help them contribute positively to the relationships, classroom ethos and wellbeing of all the children in the class. The actions taken to promote wellbeing for all children will also be of benefit to those with poor mental health.

At other times, it is a matter of understanding the nature of the difficulty that the child is having engaging in friendships, then seeking to find out a little bit about why. With this understanding, teachers can plan ways to develop specific social skills or emotional literacy or plan opportunities for these skills to be experienced and extended.

Strengths and development needs in relationships

The teacher is the most precious resource when it comes to helping children develop socially and emotionally. They set the tone in the classroom and are the role models for positive relationships. Teachers are empowering children to be able to engage in positive relationships in which their positive mental health thrives. So the teacher is facilitator, not controller or fixer.

Teacher as facilitator

- Promoting value and respect for everyone including self.
- Helping children see the good in themselves and to know that there is something good in everyone.
- Sensitive pairing of children to help strengthen friendships or social skills.
- In conflict resolution, providing opportunities and experiences that encourage the children to talk to each other when they have a disagreement. Rather than having a culture where the children come to the teacher to fix any dispute or disagreement, the teacher as facilitator will model how to resolve a situation and then encourage the children to listen to each other and come together to think of a solution, with cards or scripts as a guide initially.
- Helping the children reflect on social skills to develop further through having an academic and social learning intention and reflecting on both of these after the lesson. (This is exemplified in the next section on building good teamwork skills.)

Building good teamwork skills

In skills building, the teacher as facilitator will focus on a specific capacity, attitude or skill and help children tease out what it means. Talk about facial expression, tone of voice, body language and other ways that help children switch onto emotions and how people are feeling.

Before a task, identify together what the focus (e.g. working as part of a team) looks like and sounds like.

The children carry out the task with reminders about the focus (e.g. being a good team member).

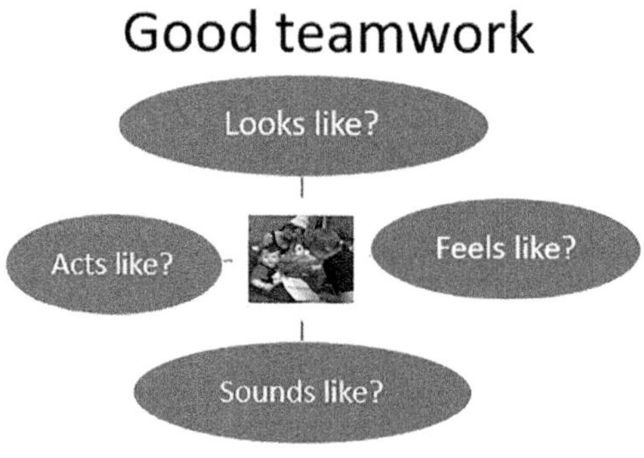

Figure 3.2 Good teamwork

Then the teacher asks the children to reflect on the focus:

- Did you experience good teamwork?
- What did it feel like?
- Did you feel included?
- Did you feel valued?
- Did you contribute to the team?
- Did you include others?
- Did you value the efforts of others?
- Was everybody positive?
- Can you give me an example of a positive word that somebody used to encourage you?
- Can you give me an example of when somebody listened to you?

Teacher as role model

Teachers should try to make explicit and voice specific social actions or emotions as they occur, as shall be discussed in more detail in Chapter 5. Even if some or all of the children are not ready to understand a specific emotion or social action in themselves or their reactions, they will remember how the teacher reacted to things, and they will be learning from seeing how the adults around them act in a range of social situations.

Mapping the social context

Sometimes a child's friendship difficulties are not immediately obvious. In addition to working to develop children's social and emotional skills and help them make friends, it is important to find out what the existing social friendship system is in the classroom. Using interviews and software to create a sociogram can be very revealing. A sociogram (Banerjee, 2010) can be created by asking the children in the class to nominate the three children they would most choose to be friends with and the three they would least choose to be friends with or three they would go to for support and three they would ask last. From this data, a social map of the classroom can be created, and it often reveals issues that the teacher has not picked up on. Please see Figure 3.3 for an example.

For example, when I first used a sociogram with my class, I found that the child most isolated was not one I would have identified. No one chose to be friendly with him, one or two thought they would go to him for support, but other than that, he had few social connections. Those children he identified as friends did not choose him in return. Without a sociogram, teachers probably could guess fairly accurately which children would come out as the so-called popular children and the children that the others might avoid. However, the sociogram might give first insight into those children who have minimal social connections - those not chosen either negatively or positively in any capacity by their peers.

When the sociogram reveals something previously unknown about peer relationships, more investigation may be needed to find out why. The child in my example was a very high-functioning intelligent only child with academic parents. He did not know how to engage lightly. His level of humour, his areas of interest and his vocabulary were completely out of

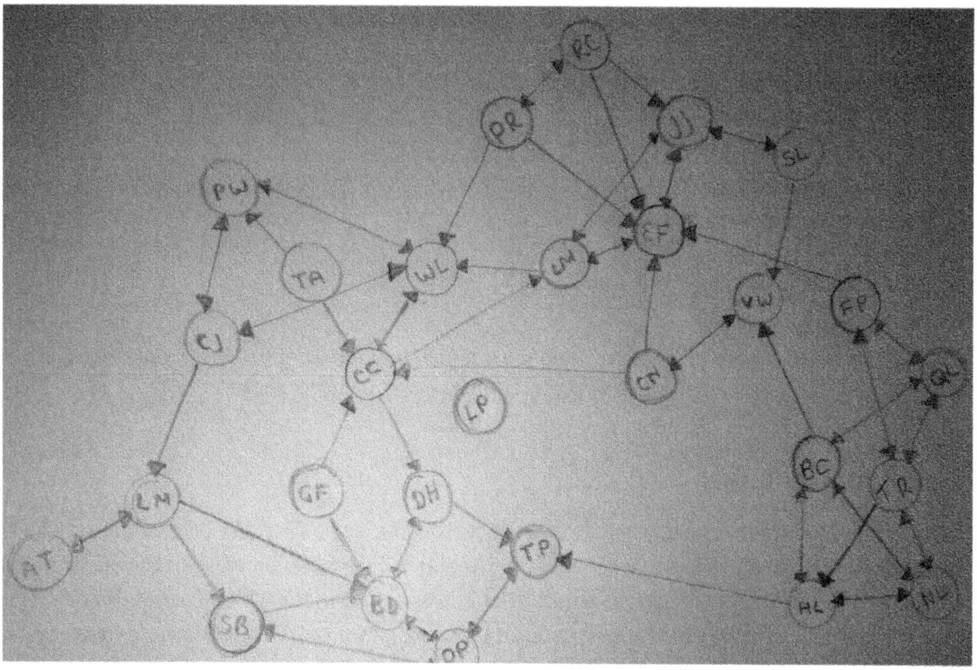

Figure 3.3 Sociogram

line with those of his peers. Taking him as an example, in order to move forward in ways that promoted his wellbeing, it was necessary to find out his perspective. Was he happy? Was he lonely, or was he completely unaware that his peers were 'missing' him, so to speak? As it stood, he was keen to have closer friendships with his peers, rather than being paired up with older children who shared his academic interests. He wanted to learn how to talk to his classmates, how to connect to them. With this in mind, we were able to implement some relevant social skills development with him and, through careful grouping and pairing, help him make closer connections to some of the classmates he wanted to befriend.

Sociograms are snapshots, and the social picture in the classroom can change rapidly and often. So, if used, they should be part of a long-term plan and updated regularly. However, the findings should always be used in conjunction with the teacher's knowledge of the child and with the child's wishes in mind. We are seeking to promote positive mental health, not to control social situations for some other purpose.

In summary, this chapter has explored the importance of:

- establishing positive relationships with pupils;
- helping the children develop their own interpersonal skills;
- knowing the children and the friendship groups well;
- the teacher as model for healthy interpersonal skills;

- the whole class environment contributing to and reinforcing the nature of positive relationships;
- the relationships between teacher and pupil and pupil and pupil, whether in the class or across the whole school, which are integral parts of the environment that promotes positive mental health;
- the frequent need for specific targeted action in the development of relationships and ethos.
- It concludes with questions from an audit to evaluate the needs and next steps for relationship building.

Audit positive relationships questions for staff

Are there any children who have difficulty making friends? How do you know?
What steps do you take to promote positive relationships?
What is your role in the children's development of social skills and positive relationships?
How well prepared do you feel for this role? Do you have any training needs?
What things about the children's interactions and relationships with each other and yourself contribute to a positive ethos?
What things about the children's interactions and relationships with each other and yourself detract from a positive ethos?
Do relationship issues (arguments/bullying/disagreements etc.) interrupt the flow of the classroom? How often? What are the issues? What might be causing these issues?
Do you take time to reflect on the children's social skills that contribute to a positive ethos?
What skills do you or the children have that contribute to a positive ethos?
What direct teaching of social and relationship skills do you do? How is this reinforced in practice?
What specific needs do the children have that might contribute to or detract from their ability to form positive relationships?

Audit questions for pupils

In your class, do you have no friends, a few friends or lots of friends?
Would you like to have more friends, the same number of friends or fewer friends?
How do you show respect to others in your class?
How do you show you are considerate of and care about other children in your class?
How do you include others?
What does valuing other children in your class look like?
In what ways do you feel respected by other children in your class?
In what ways do you feel considered/cared about by other children in your class?
In what ways do you feel included by other children in your class?
In what ways do you feel valued by other children in your class?
How do you know how to behave in your classroom?

Are there things about other children's behaviour that make you feel good?
Are there things about other children's behaviour that make you feel not so good?
How does your teacher help you get on with the others in your classroom?
Do you have someone in your classroom you trust to help you if you are unhappy or if you have a problem? Who?
Is there anything else you would like to say about friendships and getting on with other children in your class?

4 Ethos

This chapter justifies the importance of ethos to positive mental health promotion. It explores the nature of a health-promoting ethos and ways in which such an ethos can be created and maintained.

It uses scenarios and practical examples to suggest ways in which a health-promoting ethos can be created.

Quotes from primary school teachers are used to give the perspective of professionals who promote positive mental health through the creation of supportive ethos.

> *Positive mental health promotion in our school really is part of the ethos in terms of how we present ourselves, how we interact, how we value the children, the relationships we build up with them.*
>
> (Primary School Teacher)

Evaluations of positive mental health promotion initiatives identify that a whole-school supportive ethos is essential to successful promotion. There is consensus that positive mental health promotion is much more about ethos than something specifically taught. Such an ethos reflects and supports the health-promoting values and practices of the staff and pupils. The children and staff are not just talking about elements of mental health promotion; they are actually putting them into practice within an environment that supports and encourages positive mental health promotion. Hornby and Atkinson (2003) assert the need to develop an ethos in which children, school staff and parents all have and understand their roles in positive mental health promotion.

The right ethos will offer children the consistency that they need for mentally healthy development whilst also providing opportunities to experience a sense of belonging, acceptance, security and achievement (Adelman and Taylor, 2006; Oldfield, Humphrey and Hebron, 2016). Such experiences are inevitably going to have a positive impact on the child's achievement in learning as well as their mentally healthy development.

This health-promoting ethos will support a child when they experience transitions; it will enhance their social interactions and positive relationships whilst also providing social and emotional support for all those within it (Green et al., 2005; MHF, 2016).

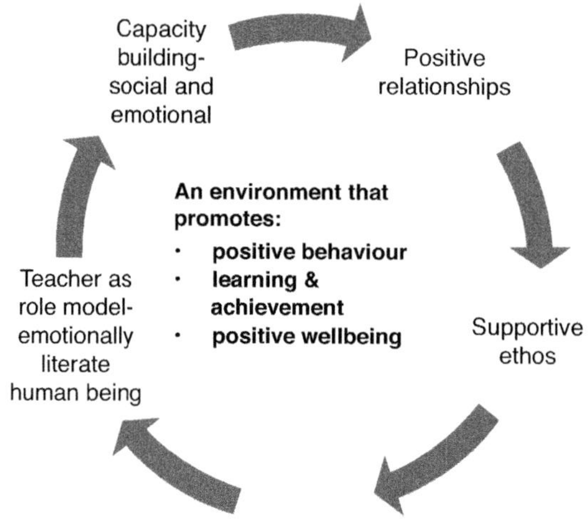

Figure 4.1 Environment that promotes positive mental health

What does a positive mental health-promoting ethos look like?

The ethos needs to be safe, respecting, supportive and inclusive. If we want a child to be able to share their emotions or discuss problems with the class, we need them to know that their contribution will be treated respectfully by the rest of the class. They will be listened to. The other children will have the skills to respond with empathy and consideration and will be encouraged to use them. Similarly, in any lesson, when a child makes a suggestion, explains their thinking or working, makes a prediction or has a try at something tricky, the ethos must be such that they feel safe to do so. They know that they will not be laughed at or mocked in any way. Clearly such an ethos is beneficial but relies on the skills of the children in the class and the teacher as positive role model. This means it may take time to get the ethos right as children are taught how to listen respectfully, accept difference and consider another child's perspective and feelings.

Praise and positive feedback promote warmth and trust. The positive reinforcement that teachers use is essential to the creation of a supportive and caring ethos. It is important to encourage and reward positive behaviour and social interactions as well as academic effort or achievement. This reinforces the underlying message that the whole child matters. In turn, this praise and positive feedback promote warmth and trust. The classroom feels like a better place to be for both children and teachers than one in which reprimands and pressure to succeed dominate.

Another characteristic of a positive classroom is the presence of fun. A recurring finding of research into positive mental health promotion is the teacher's emphasis on the importance of having fun and making being in school a positive experience. The classroom needs to be a place where both teachers and children enjoy spending time. That does not mean that everything will be fun all the time, nor is it something that can be achieved accidentally. Opportunities for fun should be planned - for example, the teacher might plan engaging and enjoyable learning activities - but they may also be spontaneous, such as the shared giggle when the whiteboard does something crazy or a joyous celebration when something goes surprisingly well. This makes the classroom a less stressful place, somewhere that laughter is possible rather than forbidden. This ethos makes the classroom a safe place in which children can thrive and learn. Enjoyment and praise also provide opportunities for emotions to be made explicit. The teacher can voice emotions and model emotional literacy. Children will learn more about their own and others' emotions through sharing these experiences.

The ethos needs to prohibit discrimination and promote equality. There has already been much written on promoting equality. However, the emphasis here is on how crucial such inclusive ways of being are to wellbeing promotion. Reciprocally, positive mental health can increase the success of actions to promote equality and reduce discrimination. Starting with work on self, respecting and valuing self, as teachers, we should work towards helping each child appreciate, respect and value their own uniqueness and differences. At the same time, we need to be increasing their awareness that everyone deserves such respect and appreciation. This can be achieved through increasing their ability to empathise and providing them with experiences that help them to see things from a variety of perspectives. A child who values self is less likely to want to exclude or hurt those who are different. A child with realistic self-esteem, life satisfaction and optimism is better able to understand and respect the needs of others, whatever their differences. They will also be able to stay safer in relationships, knowing that they are worthy of the respect, understanding and unconditional friendship of others.

The sense of ownership of and connectedness to school is enhanced by experiences that empower children, such as giving them the skills and opportunities to contribute to the whole school community and giving them a voice in school decisions (Hall, 2010). This is why it is important to involve the children in developing health-promoting strategies, to listen to them and gain their perspective whilst also helping them understand the rationale behind approaches and school or classroom codes and expectations. As is true for positive mental health promotion approaches generally, an ethos that is not informed by the child's perspective is likely to be missing something crucial. This is why the positive mental health promotion audit includes questions for children. See Appendix for full list.

Audit ethos questions for children

- What does it feel like to be in your classroom?
- Why?
- What things about your classroom or school make you feel good?
- What things about your classroom or school make you feel not so good?
- Do you always feel safe at school? Why?
- What kind of things make you feel safe at school?
- What kinds of things make you feel less safe at school?
- What do you do if you have a problem in class?
- Is there someone you would ask for help if you needed it?

There are many ways to gather the children's perspectives on the classroom, depending on their age and how accustomed they are to consultation. Their views might be gathered through the written questions listed earlier, through a conversation or by asking the children to respond to the questions with pictures. A sense of belonging is crucial to positive mental health. Not every child will find it easy to connect. This is why it is so important to know the children in your class well, to find ways to connect to them and help them engage. If every child has the opportunity to feed into plans to promote positive mental health, they will have more ownership but only if they feel their voice has been heard and not ignored.

When getting the children's perspective through an audit such as this, try to address something raised by every child rather than going for the majority all the time. There may be small changes that can be made to support an individual child to feel safer and included, even if it is out of line with the needs of the whole class: for example, seating them near the door if they express discomfort at having to walk past all the other children to go to the toilet. Teacher response to an audit can also reinforce the ethos of diversity, valuing differences and the different needs and wants they bring. This can build children's awareness that whilst they might like or dislike something, another child might feel very differently about it.

Another way to increase a sense of belonging and connectedness to school and the classroom is when the school staff take opportunities to chat with children, to eat lunch with them and join in their conversations. This allows the children to see the staff as real people, and if they lead the casual conversations, what they bring is being valued. They can mention something they have done outside school or something in which they are interested and have that aspect of their lives acknowledged. Shared meals or snacks can also provide opportunities to emphasise the sense of family or school community. Children who have a sense of belonging are usually more secure. This secure base allows them to be more welcoming and inclusive of others.

As you can see, there is a great deal of overlap between the different characteristics of a health-promoting ethos and the ways to promote them. The elements of ethos discussed so far will foster the positive relationships between school staff, children and families that were discussed in Chapter 3. It is also iterative: such an ethos promotes positive mental health, and the mentally healthy characteristics, in turn, increase the success of the supportive health-promoting ethos. Rather than being constructed, the ethos grows and evolves, influenced by those within it as this teacher's comment illustrates:

> I think that would be fair to say that the ethos can't be contrived because if you try to engineer it, it all goes pear shaped. I think it really has to be something that evolves; it's organic and natural – a natural equilibrium that is established. It's just how we are.

In summary, an ethos that promotes positive mental health will have the following characteristics:

- safe,
- respecting,
- inclusive,
- supportive,
- equal,
- positive toward relationships,
- consistent,
- caring,

- encouraging empathy and emotional literacy,
- empowering,
- engendering of ownership and connectedness.

The health-promoting ethos will be enhanced by emotionally literate teachers (Hornby and Atkinson, 2003) and other adults who act as role models for the ethos-creating behaviours and attitudes.

And it will seek to remove barriers to mental health promotion, such as:

- discrimination,
- conflict,
- bullying,
- mixed messages/inconsistency.

Challenges

Consistency

Whole-school policies should be consistent with health promotion strategies and provide consistency across the school. A shared vision gives all staff understanding of positive mental health promotion and how it permeates everything that they do: for example, the presence of a school focus on positive reinforcement and a school-wide way of relating to pupils. This means that children know they will get a consistent response wherever they are; success and achievement will be celebrated at every level, and each adult will greet a child in a similar way. The latter is acknowledged in this teacher's comments:

> When the children are walking along the corridor, every adult will say something to them such as, 'Oh good morning, Phoebe'. The children will go, 'Good morning', and as soon as you smile at them, they smile back. It's our culture.

However, it takes time to embed such consistency of approach across a school. You need the understanding and investment of all school staff, which is harder if the promotion approaches are vastly different from a school's existing ethos or a teacher's vision for teaching. It is not necessarily a matter of adding health-promoting strategies to an existing ethos. Sometimes there will be policies and school aims that seem to be incompatible with the positive mental health- promoting ethos: for example, ones focused on attainment in tests or school position in league tables. In such cases, the whole school team needs to come together to work out how to help every child achieve their potential within a health-promoting environment. Such work benefits from the consideration of the purpose of teaching previously mentioned in Chapter 3. In order to help colleagues understand the importance and value of positive mental health promotion, it can be useful to look at the benefits to a child's academic attainment of positive mental health promotion strategies and at the correlation between positive mental health promotion and learning discussed in Chapter 2. Strategies for developing a whole-school approach to positive mental health promotion are discussed in Chapter 8.

Working with children who experience poor mental health

Positive mental health promotion seeks to help as many children as possible experience positive mental health most of the time. It is intended to make school a healthier experience for all and reduce the number of children experiencing poor mental health. However, currently, mental health problems in children and adolescents are increasing (Murphy, 2016); one in eight children in the UK (one in ten in Scotland) have mental health difficulties (Office for National Statistics, 2015). It is much harder to foster and maintain a health-promoting ethos when there are a significant number of children whose mental health is not good. It is hard to get the positive reinforcement and atmosphere when a class contains children whose behaviour is influenced by social and emotional difficulties, trauma or poor attachment, for example.

The children who most need a strong positive relationship with teachers and classmates are often those for whom such relationships are hardest to establish. They will, however, benefit from the health-promoting ethos, and with consistent positive reinforcement of the expectations and some targeted health promotion interventions, every child will be able to contribute positively in some way to the ethos, even if not all the time. Many books have been written on working with children with social and emotional difficulties, and there is no intention to repeat the good work here. What is important is to acknowledge that the presence of children with poor mental health will make creating a positive, safe and supportive ethos that much harder, but not impossible. It will involve collaboration with other professionals and partnership with parents. It will take its toll on the teacher, and this element of positive mental health promotion is explored in Chapter 9.

Positive mental health promotion across the whole school day

There can be points in a school day at which it is harder to achieve a supportive ethos. Playtimes and lunchtimes are often cited as sources of disputes and unhappiness, with some teachers claiming that they spend a significant amount of time after each break helping children deal with the issues that have arisen during their play. This is where consistent approaches to positive reinforcement and conflict resolution, combined with a school-wide emphasis on emotional literacy and calming strategies, become invaluable. Some schools find that their positive mental health promotion initiatives need to start with the playground. Others find it useful to display reminders of calming strategies or conflict resolution in play and lunch areas and to equip supervising staff with prompt cards. These difficulties make it very clear that everyone in the school, whatever their role, needs to be on board with the promotion strategies. Everyone needs to understand what to do and why and to be invested in each approach used. The staff, whether teachers, school leaders, play- or lunchtime supervisors, all need to be actively involved in promotion so that they can make sure their responses are consistent with school ethos and to help reinforce the sense of stability.

So far, this chapter has considered the importance and rationale for a health-promoting ethos. It will now present some approaches and suggestions for taking this forward in the classroom, with the caveat that the approaches each teacher chooses have to meet the needs of the children, school and context in order to be most effective. We also need to believe in what we are doing if we truly want to have positive impact.

Where to start?

Work to promote positive relationships as discussed in Chapter 3 will contribute to the creation of a supportive safe ethos. The next steps are to get to know the children and to use this knowledge to make sure that the ethos accommodates their needs and provides opportunities for further mentally healthy development. Easier said than done? The ethos will be unique to the teacher and the pupils, so a step-by-step guide to ethos creation cannot be given here. What follows instead are examples and recommendations from teachers and evaluations of practice.

A culture of talking

There needs to be a culture where children feel they are in a trusted environment so that they can speak honestly and say how they feel and why they feel that way. Such a culture will come with the positive relationships previously mentioned and will rely on the consistent demonstration of positive regard and empathy from the class teacher, who should model these ways of being and make explicit what they are doing so that the children notice and learn. For example:

Child: I don't want to go. I hate football.
Teacher: You hate football! Wow. That surprises me because I love football. Can you tell us a little bit more about why you hate it?
Child: It is scary, and everyone shouts a lot.
Teacher: I am sorry that it scares you. When I am scared, I try to think of something else, something that I like. What do you do when you are scared?
Child: I want to go home.
Teacher: How about everyone else? What do you do when something is noisy and scary? How do you cope?

In this example, the teacher is valuing the child's perspective, making explicit their own different perspective and showing interest in why the child has this perspective. The expressed 'hate' is not dismissed or judged, but the feelings behind it are explored, and the rest of the class are invited to talk about coping strategies that they have. This helps the first child feel part of a group who also feel scared at times. No one is telling the child that they have to master their fear, but they are exploring ways that other children do so to reveal the possibility that we can do scary things sometimes, and it can even bring rewards, such as a sense of achievement.

The teacher is an important role model in this dialogue, making explicit emotions and facilitating the continued conversation. The way that the teacher responds to the first child and the subsequent contributions of others sets the tone for the discussion. They are a positive model for respect. They should positively reinforce the value of constructive comments and pick up on any which are insensitive or approaching cruel:

Child 2: Ha ha. Fancy being scared of football.
Teacher: Do we laugh at other people's feelings? Is it helpful?
Child 2: No, but . . .
Teacher: What scares you? How can you help Ethan come out to watch the football? What do you do when you are scared?

This modelling and reinforcement are things that we do all the time as teachers. It is an important part of a supportive and safe ethos and should not be undervalued. Effective teachers make use of opportunities that present themselves throughout the school day and use these to model emotional literacy and care or to reinforce the feeling of the supportive safe ethos. That said, it is not possible to stop and engage in discussion on every grumble, fear or challenge. What is important is to acknowledge the issue and, if possible, use a set time of the day or week to come back to it and engage with it in more depth: for example, in circle time, solution circles etc.

It is OK to get it wrong

Once you have begun to create a culture in which it is safe to talk, children will also be more confident voicing their ideas and difficulties when working on a task. Along with positive regard, there should be an encouragement to try, a valuing of learning through experience, through trial and error: that is, a destigmatising of failure or getting something wrong. Children need academic as well as social and emotional resilience. It can often be the most able children who struggle the most with challenge and not getting something quite how they want it the first time. Yet if we do not give them opportunities for trial and error, they will never develop these skills and resilience. To support this aspect of a health-promoting ethos, teachers can keep reminding children that it is good to try and that it is OK to get something wrong. Working things out together and exploring strategies in maths and making predictions in science provide opportunities to value learning from mistakes or reviewing and trying again. These are things most primary school teachers will be doing anyway. It is then just a matter of making it explicit, valuing suggestions and attempts as much as the solution.

Child 1: I think it will float now we have plugged the hole with paper.
Teacher: That is a sensible prediction. Let's see what happens.
Child 1: Oh, it still isn't floating.
Teacher: Well, that was useful to try. We have learned that it still sinks if we put paper in the hole. I wonder why?
Child 2: Look, the paper got wet and tore.
Teacher: Well spotted.
Child 3: Paper isn't waterproof.
Teacher: Good point. How do we use this to help us have another try?

Another way in which to emphasise the value of learning from mistakes and to reduce fear of failure is for the teacher to voice it when they get something wrong or to model what they might do. Explain how you remember a certain spelling or formula; get the dictionary out to look up a tricky spelling or say I don't know and look up something you don't know. As a teacher, I have found my clumsiness with anything arty to be a great way to do model trial and error. I would attempt to draw something we needed on the whiteboard. The children would see that, actually, they could probably have done a better job. I would voice my dissatisfaction:

Teacher: Oh dear. I haven't managed to get that house right. How can I make it better?

I would then allow the children to give me advice on how to make the house look more realistic. There would be no laughter at the attempt, no belittling, just constructive comments on what was not quite right and how to make it better. It is essential to be striving for better and not perfection, so the children would often be heard saying later, 'That was quite good for Miss Holt. It looks a bit like a house now'. Not only does such an approach help reduce fear of trying something; it also helps build confidence and self-esteem. If the teacher needs help sometimes, then it must be OK.

Class codes involving positive reinforcement and the absence of demonising

Having a class behaviour or learning code that the children draw up together and reinforce positively as a class is another effective way to create a health-promoting ethos. When children have ownership and understanding of the behavioural and learning expectations in the classroom, they will be more likely to behave in sociable and supportive ways. If, alongside the teacher, they have a role in recognising strengths and helpful acts in their classmates, there will be much more positive reinforcement and motivation to support and consider each other. They will be working for themselves and for their friends, not for some abstract rule. They will be reluctant to let the class or the teacher down because they have this investment in the class code. As positive reinforcement is a common approach in primary schools now, this element of creating a mentally healthy ethos is something every teacher probably already has experience of - another element of promotion that teachers are already doing anyway.

When children know that they can come back from a slip in expected behaviour (the avoidance of demonising or labelling as discussed in the positive regard section of Chapter 3), it is less likely to have a detrimental impact on their wellbeing and behaviour. They know that it is the behaviour that has been identified as a problem, not them. They know that they still have a chance to turn things around and make a positive contribution, making it more likely that they will do so. A minor slip does not shatter the class ethos.

Care and nurture

One of the integral elements of a supportive ethos is care. This includes the care teachers have for their pupils and their work, the care children have for each other and the class and the emphasis on caring that is present in the classroom. The positive relationships discussed in the previous chapter both increase the sense of care and are enhanced by being in a caring environment. This is easier to achieve when class sizes are smaller, but there are still ways to find time to have a positive interaction with each child at least once a day. A caring ethos can be demonstrated through the way the teacher greets each child when they come into school in the mornings and the ways in which the children welcome each other.

Whether following official Nurture Group Principles (Bennathan and Boxall, 2000) or just taking a general nurturing approach, many schools incorporate nurture into their mental health promotion strategies. In addition to showing the care and positive relationships of a caring ethos, nurture will also include providing opportunities for children's healthy social development. In some cases, this means taking time from the busy school day to sit at a table in the classroom and eat toast together or share a drink and have a chat. The school staff model socially healthy behaviours at the meal table, encouraging sharing and taking turns listening and talking.

If children routinely come into school unsettled after a weekend or every weekday, it can be a good idea to schedule time in the day for chatting or checking in. This is not like the 'news' sessions that used to take place where children have to sit for an extended time while one child speaks at a time. If they are unsettled and full of nervous energy, a more active and fluid catch-up is required, where children can wander around the room talking to each other, while the staff also try to check in with as many children as necessary. When a teacher knows the children well, it is often quite easy for them to notice if there is something wrong. This informal time allows opportunities for teachers to notice such children and ask them if they want to talk. Plan to have the first 30 minutes on a Monday morning set aside for informal chats and catching up about the weekend and perhaps a good ten minutes every morning. A worry box fits quite well into this approach. At this informal time of coming and going, a child can make a note for the worry box (or, if they are young, find their name card and post that in the worry box). This allows them an element of control, a way to indicate to their teacher that they have something on their mind. Even the act of posting the worry can free a child up to think about other things, be that school work or something social, safe in the knowledge that their worry will be picked up later in the day.

Specific calming strategies

It is sometimes immediately evident that the class as a whole would benefit from specific techniques embedded within the day to help everyone contribute to and benefit from the safe supportive ethos.

Calming

It can be helpful to teach the children calming strategies or to help each child work out what they can do to help them calm themselves when they are distracted by a strong emotion. Excitement and joy, anger and sadness, envy and fear can stop a child from being able to participate in group work, concentrate on their solo work or even engage in conversation with others. If every child has a calming strategy that works for them, the reminder to use their calming strategy can be embedded into the school day. First, there needs to be specific lessons or circle time on emotions and a sharing of the way each child manages their behaviour when experiencing a specific emotion. (More on emotional literacy is discussed in Chapter 5, where it is made clear that managing an emotion is not suppressing it.) Each child should explore what works best for them. Whilst the children discover ways to manage a strong emotion, they are also learning about other children, reinforcing attitudes and acceptance and recognising and valuing diversity. Calming strategies can vary greatly and are best worked out by the child rather than imposed on them. Personally, every time I engage in or observe such activities or interview teachers about this, I discover a new strategy that works for an individual.

Teachers can help children identify two or three calming strategies and record these in writing or pictures on laminated cards that they can display or use to communicate their situation if required. At other times a teacher might ask the child to choose one of their calming strategies or cards as a reminder to walk away from a situation or to help them avoid an escalation.

Some immediately obvious strategies include:

- counting to 10,
- counting backwards from 100,
- thinking of a sunny day,
- taking three deep breaths,
- listening to calming music,
- clenching and relaxing your muscles.

There are others that may be more specific to a child's needs, such as:

- waking away,
- running around the playground,
- talking to the class puppet or mascot/recording a message to the class friend/writing a letter to someone,
- cuddling the teddy,
- imagining you are building a model car and thinking about where all the pieces go,
- remembering the lyrics to a favourite song,
- retelling a story in your head,
- working out the seven-times table.

As you can see, some strategies involve what we might consider to be actions that calm us such as deep breaths and soothing thoughts, but sometimes distraction is needed. Children frequently say deep breaths do not help. 'What use is counting? I'm still angry/scared/excited'. However, after doing something to distract them, be it physical or mental, the children may then feel calmer or more receptive to soothing thoughts or positive solutions.

These calming strategies embedded within the classroom or whole school can make a significant contribution to the safe and supportive ethos. However, they should not be used instead of helping the children talk about and process their emotions. This emotional processing is still a valuable part of positive mental health promotion and is explored in more detail in Chapter 5.

Other effective ways to contribute to a health-promoting ethos are to incorporate elements of yoga, mindfulness or other relaxation sessions into the school day. At the other extreme are activities such as the daily mile or school walk, where children experience the mental and physical benefits of a short burst of structured physical activity at some point each day.

Calming strategies are all relative, and it may take time to move from something aggressive to something more consistent with a safe space. One example of this is the child who used to lash out, hitting and kicking anyone near when he was angry, scared, excited or upset:

Child: Miss, Miss, I am getting better at not hurting people when I am upset.
Teacher: That's good. Tell me a bit more about that.
Child: I was really cross, but I didn't hit anyone, I just kicked the chairs. Isn't that good?
Teacher: That is much better than hurting someone. Well done. What else could you do next time?

This child is on the slow but steady path from aggression against others to more socially acceptable and safe ways of expressing and dealing with his emotions. This might be extreme in another child, but this child had taken the first step in moving from people to chairs. It would be a while before he would benefit from a standard calming strategy, but his actions showed understanding, awareness and a desire to change the way he managed his feelings. The teacher's receptive response would make all the difference. She recognised his efforts rather than only seeing the kicked chairs. This example also illustrates the importance of school staff knowing all the children well and being able to recognise atypical positive steps.

The change in one child can make a difference in how safe every child in the class feels.

Reinforcement of ethos

An ethos that promotes positive mental health is multifaceted and will usually take time to achieve. It is almost inseparable from the other elements of positive mental health promotion because it reinforces them whilst also relying on them. Many elements of ethos are dependent on the relationships within the school, the children's social and emotional skills and development and consistent demonstration of values, such as respect and positive regard.

The ethos relies on the individuals within each class and school. The teacher is responsible for organising the classroom sensitively and serves as a positive role model, both making explicit and reinforcing desired behaviours and attitudes throughout each day.

When reading this book, it is recommended that each of the chapters is considered in relation to another. Positive mental health promotion is complicated and best achieved little by little according to priorities. Consider:

- What are the needs in the school?
- Which elements of ethos, positive relationships, empowerment and emotional literacy are priorities for the children in your class?
- Which specific skills and experiences are needed to address the priority needs?

- Then, rather than addressing one element (chapter) at a time, use relevant elements from each chapter to support implementation of a new approach or review of existing practice. The audit and professional learning tasks in the Appendix should assist with this.

Concluding comments

Ethos is illusive and unique. Each teacher needs to work out what it means for them in their classroom with their class. That is why this chapter begins and ends with a teacher's comments on their thoughts on the role of ethos in positive mental health promotion.

The following description of positive mental health promotion exemplifies the way in which ethos and emotional literacy are integral parts of the classroom climate:

> Positive mental health to us is an environment where the children are emotionally literate; they can express their pleasures, their anxieties; they can know what to do if they are feeling certain things. It's getting that culture of 'we can talk about these things'; we don't pretend they don't exist.

In summary, this chapter has:

- presented the rationale for ethos as a way to promote positive mental health;
- discussed characteristics of a health-promoting ethos: safe, respecting, supportive, inclusive, equality, positive toward relationships, consistent, caring, encouraging empathy and emotional literacy, empowering, engendering ownership and connectedness;
- emphasised the ways to include children in the process;
- looked at ways in which a supportive ethos can be created.

It concludes with questions for an audit to evaluate the needs and next steps for ethos creation.

Audit ethos questions for school staff

School ethos

What does it feel like to work in your school?
Why might this be?
Is there anything that could be improved about the school ethos/environment to make it feel a better place to work? If so, what could be done? What would make it feel a better place to work?
Do you have colleagues you trust to confide in?
Do you feel supported in your role? Why?
What would make you feel more supported?

Classroom ethos

What does it feel like to be in your classroom? Why?
Do you know how the children feel about their classroom?

Thinking of the physical environment

Which aspects do you think contribute to creating a safe and positive ethos?
Which aspects might make it a less safe or positive ethos?

Thinking of the social and emotional environment

Which elements do you think contribute to a positive ethos?
Which elements detract from a positive ethos?
How often do the children smile and laugh in the classroom?
Do the children look relaxed/content/secure?
How do the children treat each other?
How well do the children collaborate?
Do the children show respect to each other (and you)?
Do the children show care for others? How?
Do the children express concerns or difficulties?

Audit Questions for pupils appear earlier in this chapter.

5 Emotional literacy

In this chapter:

There is discussion of the rationale and theory base for emotional literacy, drawing on relevant literature.

Emotional literacy is defined, and practical illustrations are given to exemplify.

The role of the teacher and the importance of teacher as role model are explored.

Examples and scenarios are used to provide practical examples of some of the many ways in which teachers can contribute to pupils' emotional literacy development.

There are many good texts on emotional literacy, and I recommend that, for detailed consideration of emotional literacy, these should also be consulted. The purpose of this chapter is to highlight key elements of emotional literacy and why and how the development of emotional literacy is an integral part of positive mental health promotion.

Rationale

If, as discussed in Chapter 1, positive mental health includes the ability to develop emotionally and socially, then emotional literacy is an important part of this development. There are claims that increased emotional literacy reduces depressive symptoms (Perry, Lennie and Humphrey, 2008; Wright et al., 2010). Emotional literacy has also been found to reduce some of the risk factors that demote positive mental health such as self-destructive or risk-taking behaviours (Banerjee, 2010; Perry, Lennie and Humphrey, 2008; Wright et al., 2010). Some evaluations have found that emotional literacy enhances achievement, but this is hard to measure and so is often discounted for lack of quantifiable evidence (Walberg, Zins and Weissberg, 2004). Evaluations of successful positive mental health promotion identify the importance of teachers who are nonjudgemental, who listen carefully to the children's feelings and problems, value them and respond empathically and sensitively.

Social and emotional development

Two of the core elements of positive mental health are social and emotional development. These aspects are so interconnected that whilst we can define them separately, they are usually considered together. The boundaries and distinctions between can be quite fluid. Drawing from the work of other specialists in this field, these bullet points present some of the ways social and emotional development are connected:

- Children learn about themselves and their own emotions by being in relationships with others (Denzin, 1984; Thompson, 2007).
- By being in relationships with others, children come into contact with the emotions of others (Denzin, 1984; Thompson, 2007).
- A child's social development includes the awareness of others (Zeidner, Roberts and Matthews, 2002).
- Empathy, a capacity associated with emotional development, is an attribute counted when social wellbeing is measured (Bradshaw and Tipping, 2010).

Empathy

When working to promote positive mental health, it is worth reviewing your own conception of empathy. It is beneficial if school teams can come to a shared understanding of the term. Sometimes it helps to start with what it is not.

Empathy is not:

- sympathy,
- remembering how you felt when the same thing happened to you,
- imagining how you would feel.

So now we know what empathy is not. How can we define, understand and nurture it? Although not new, Rogers's (1967) useful definition of empathy is 'the walking in another's shoes and understanding that other person's emotions even if they are different from those you would experience' (1967).

Goroshit and Hen (2016) add that empathy also involves appropriate emotional response through the expression of understanding. It is not enough to be aware of someone else's feelings; empathy involves communicating your understanding to them in some way. This is how empathy contributes to our own and others' positive mental health as well as being a characteristic of emotional literacy. Empathy enriches relationships and is enriched by them (Hargreaves, 2005; Rogers, 1967).

However, teachers cannot teach children to feel empathy. Nor can teachers (or any adult) go on a course and return qualified in empathy. Empathy is a feeling and a connection. It can be expressed through body language and actions as well as in words. Goroshit and Hen (2016) argue that this communication of empathy is what strengthens positive relationships. In school, rather than seeking to teach empathy, teachers can set out to teach children how to respond with empathy and how to behave in empathetic ways. At the same time, they can be helping children develop their emotional literacy by providing opportunities for them to experience and observe empathy and engage in positive relationships.

As you can see, in these ways, emotional literacy depends on relationships, and positive relationships thrive on emotional literacy. When we work in schools to establish positive relationships, we may need to begin with identifying and then helping children develop any emotional literacy skills that are not yet evident in the classroom. A child will learn about self through being in relationships with others (Denzin, 1984; Silverman, 2012). In order to understand and begin to have empathy for another person, a child needs to have some understanding of their own emotions. That is emotional literacy.

Defining emotional literacy

Emotional literacy is generally considered to involve:

- self-understanding;
- recognising and experiencing a range of emotions;
- understanding the causes and deciding how to act;
- understanding social situations;
- expressing emotions appropriately;
- recognising emotions in others and experiencing empathy;
- developing relationships;
- using these for the benefit of others, not just for self.

(Morris and Scott, 2003; Perry, Lennie and Humphrey, 2008; Weare, 2010; Zeidner, Roberts and Matthews, 2002).

There is no single descriptor for an emotionally literate child. Each child will differ, and their emotional literacy will change and develop over time. It might become more sophisticated with maturity, but it is also likely to weaken in times of stress or loss or when relationships are fractured (Mental Health Foundation (MHF), 2016). Emotional literacy might be evidenced in the way children engage in positive relationships, manage conflict and other tricky situations or in the way they demonstrate empathy towards each other (Kelly et al., 2004; Weare, 2010).

Caution

If schools and teachers are going to model and foster a child's development of emotional literacy as part of their work on positive mental health promotion, it is useful to look at some of the concerns and issues related to emotional literacy so that they can be recognised and avoided.

- Emotional literacy is **not** a focus on the so-called positive emotions to the exclusion of all others.
- It is **not** the regulation or suppressing of emotions.
- The teacher's role is **not** one of training children to experience only certain feelings.

- Emotional literacy development needs to be addressed as one of many elements of positive mental health promotion and not the only approach.

Instead, emotional literacy requires a focus on reflection and self-awareness. This means being able to recognise the emotions one is experiencing, so that there is the ownership and understanding of those emotions (Morris and Scott, 2003; Weare, 2010). Such recognition of one's own emotions reduces the chance of the emotions being projected onto someone else.

Scenario 1: The child's emotional literacy

For example, take the child – let's call her Annabel – who feels hate and anger towards another child (Oscar) to the point where she can or wants to act aggressively towards that other child. Annabel is repeatedly blaming someone else for the way that she feels and wants to hurt them to get rid of these feelings. Reflection and understanding of her feelings could help Annabel behave differently and increase the possibility that she might feel better. In this particular example, Annabel needs support from the teacher to work out specifically what is causing her deep feelings. This does not mean that the teacher is expecting Annabel to repress her feelings. Through dialogue, talk and play, social stories or even role play with the teacher or someone in whom Annabel can confide, it emerges that Oscar is going on holiday, and Annabel is upset because she is not going on holiday this year. What she feels is sadness about not having a holiday and very strong jealousy of Oscar, who is going on holiday. Oscar's excitement about his holiday has increased Annabel's sadness and made her feel very jealous of Oscar. Until she worked through her feelings in conversation with the teacher or trusted adult, she had not realised the connection between her hatred and anger towards Oscar and her sadness about the holiday. This greater self-understanding has the potential to help Annabel change her behaviour, leaving opportunities for discussion of coping strategies (one to one or part of a whole class).

The following could be explored through role play, solution circles or engagement with some of the many children's texts that cover such emotions.

- How do the children cope when they can't have what they want?
- How do they cope when someone else has something they want?
- What can they do to feel better?

The situation could then be extended fully to consider the others within the relationship:

- How does Oscar feel?
- How would he feel if the roles were reversed?
- Would he want to change his behaviour now that he knows of Annabel's sadness and jealousy? Should he?
- What can others do to support someone feeling this way?
- How do we manage our response to the excitement, pride or enthusiasm of others, particularly when it reminds us of our own difference?

There is so much potential in this scenario to help all the children in the class understand their own emotions, the way they respond to them and how these responses affect others. It is used here to illustrate the value of emotional literacy and its embeddedness within relationships.

Scenario 2: The emotionally literate teacher

Teachers also need to develop their own emotional literacy and make sure that they can identify their feelings. Think of the days when you are stressed, for example, because the headteacher is coming to observe a lesson later in the day. The children seem bouncier, less focused, louder, more argumentative than usual. You feel annoyed with them for being like this when you really need them on their best behaviour.

Before going any further - stop! Two things could be going on here, simultaneously or singly:

1 Are the children really the cause of your annoyance and irritation?

   It may just be that the children are the same as usual, but your expectations have changed because you are stressed and anxious. Will it help your situation if you misinterpret your anxiety as anger/frustration or irritation at the children?

2 Are your stress and anxiety transmitting to the children?

   In trying to bottle up or ignore your own feelings of anxiety or stress, you might still be conveying these feelings to the children subconsciously. The children, feeling unsettled, then try to seek reassurance through less productive ways of behaving.

The most productive way through this situation would be to focus on your feelings. Work out how you can manage to get through the day whilst experiencing those feelings without them triggering a downward spiral of events. Many teachers, myself included, find an effective way through this is to be honest with the children.

> Mrs Pride is coming to watch us work this afternoon, and that is making me feel a bit nervous as if I was going to have a test this afternoon. Can you imagine how I might be feeling? I think I might need a bit of help from you to help me feel less nervous. What can we do to help us all feel calm and relaxed today?

An emotionally literate teacher will recognise their feelings and so, with this recognition, can take responsibility for them and act on them. This is in contrast to the teacher who blames the children for the way the teacher is feeling.

Emotional literacy includes a level of emotional reflexivity. Children and teachers will inevitably bring their emotions into the classroom. It is this emotional reflexivity that helps teachers understand their own feelings and the impact of their emotions on their pupils. If teachers do not have a close relationship with the children in their class, they can misunderstand the emotions of the children (Denzin, 1984), as this teacher explained:

> I know if I am feeling vulnerable, I am more likely to misunderstand a child's emotional needs, or I might even not notice there is something wrong.

Valuing all feelings

From these two examples of the child and the teacher, it becomes clear how, through the development of emotional literacy, feelings can be recognised and managed in self and others (Morris and Scott, 2003; Weare, 2010). However, this does not mean that so-called negative emotions are demonized or that these are the only emotions that can result in antisocial or impulsive behaviour. I can certainly recall many occasions when my lessons were disturbed by excitedly happy children. Rather, emotional literacy means that an individual recognises how they are feeling, whatever the nature of that feeling, and begins to get a better understanding of why they feel that way and what they need to do to deal with it, rather than acting on an impulse triggered by the emotion. Such emotional competence can increase the sense of life satisfaction in addition to serving as a coping strategy. (Goroshit and Hen, 2016).

Using emotional literacy development to promote positive mental health

The teacher

The teacher's role in emotional literacy development is a personal one because it relies on the emotions of the teacher and how these are managed in the teacher's professional life. It relies on the teacher's:

- awareness of their own feelings,
- emotional response to situations,
- awareness of the potential impact of their response on the feelings of the children,
- ability and confidence to seize opportunities to share their feelings and responses in ways that help children develop their own emotional literacy.

Emotionally literate teachers are defined as having self-knowledge; they understand their own feelings and are aware of those of their pupils. They listen to and have empathy for their pupils.

Emotionally literate teachers value the place of emotion in the classroom. They encourage children to acknowledge and learn to understand their feelings about their learning or school friendships.

Emotionally literate or empathic teachers are also better able to foster a sense of community and belonging in the classroom (Goroshit and Hen, 2016; Mental Health Foundation, 2016). They make a significant contribution to positive mental health promotion.

Role model

I am sure no teacher reading this book needs to be told that teachers need patience. However, teachers are human beings and will inevitably experience impatience or frustration on occasions. One teacher explained how they manage such feelings productively:

> If a child for whatever reason has caused you to be impatient, rather than displaying that verbally or bodily, you need to take a breath, take time and respond fairly or explain that you will get back to them in a minute.

If the teacher's behaviour remains calm, the ethos in the classroom is maintained, and there is time to frame an appropriate, calm but fair response to the child.

In this way, a teacher can draw on their own social skills to create a climate in which children value and respect each other. Every minute in the classroom, the teacher is a role model for emotional literacy and positive mental health. The children will respond to what they are seeing. Even if they do not understand their own feelings and response, they can observe the teacher and remember how they react to things. Children learn as much about social and emotional development from how a teacher behaves as they do from what the teacher says. Being a role model for positive mental health through demonstrating emotional literacy contributes to the positive relationship between teacher and pupils. This supports academic development as well as healthy social and emotional development (Biesta, 2016; Cooper, 2010; Pantić and Wubbels, 2012).

Thus we return to the importance of the teacher as a human being that was highlighted in Chapter 3. In order to be a role model for emotional literacy, a teacher has to be a real person to the children. They have to let the children see their human side. This can be demonstrated through a specific modelling of emotional literacy.

Disappointment

For example, when dealing with a behaviour issue, the teacher might say to the class, 'Can you see I am disappointed?' When saying this, the teacher will emphasise the tone of voice relevant to a feeling of disappointment. They will make sure that their facial expression also shows this feeling. The teacher is conveying the feeling through words, tone of voice and facial cues. Eventually, the children will begin to recognise when they feel disappointed and will have a positive model for how to express it.

Hope and belief

Teachers with hope and belief in what they are doing are better able to nurture hope in their pupils (Bullough, 2011). Naming of characteristics and emotions such as hope can make it easier for children to acquire them (Bullough, 2011).

> I am feeling hopeful. I believe that the infants are going to love our assembly.

This gives the children a living example of that emotion. In sharing emotions such as hope, the teacher is also modelling a characteristic of and contributor to positive mental health. Hope or optimism that things will improve can help children and adults cope with difficult times. It supports resilience.

Making a point

Teachers have daily opportunities to model how it is possible to get their point across while being calm and in control, without shouting or losing their temper. Every now and then, it is necessary to make this explicit to the children.

> Did you notice then that I had a different opinion on the Vikings from Georgina?
> How did I show this?
> Did I shout at her and tell her she was wrong? Did I lose my temper?
> No – so what did I do?
> That's right. We both listened to each other's opinions calmly. I now understand Georgina's opinion, but I haven't changed mine, and that feels OK.

I got it wrong

When trying to foster an ethos of learning through making mistakes, the teacher's modelling of how this is done and the feelings involved is invaluable. It can be tough to do. It takes confidence and it might leave the teacher feeling vulnerable at first, but it usually strengthens relationships with pupils as well as helping the children understand their own feelings around getting something wrong. It is easier to do in relation to academic learning:

> Oh look, I have spelt that word wrong. I think I must have got the e and the i the wrong way around. What do you think?
> Let's swap them around.
> Does that look right now? I think so but maybe we should check.
> How could we check?

However, if the teacher can also model this in social or emotional situations it helps the children see them as a person and value them more.

> OK, maybe I shouldn't have been quite so hard.
> On reflection, I feel that wasn't fair.
> I am sorry about that.

In this way, through their honest actions, apologies and the related discussion of emotions, teachers can model how to repair difficult situations. They show that it is human to get impatient or angry. Such openness around mistakes and recovery can also help reduce any stigma or shame that might be associated with getting it wrong, either academically or socially.

Seizing opportunities

The children's emotional literacy will be supported significantly if the teacher is able to voice and make explicit any emotion provoked by a classroom experience.

Teacher:	*Oh, George. That is fantastic! You read that story to me* (tears rolling down face).
Other children:	*You're crying, Miss.*
Teacher:	*I am happy and proud because George has just started to read for the first time which is really, really good. Let's all stop and give him a cheer. Well done, George.*

This demonstration and explanation of feelings is particularly helpful because it may be the first time the children have considered tears as something joyful. In this example, it was in response to the children's questions, but it can also be initiated by the teacher. If we are going to make emotional literacy development meaningful and relevant, it requires having the confidence or judgement to stop a lesson and address a particular issue while it is meaningful and relevant to the children, rather than leaving it for a health and wellbeing or PSHE lesson:

Voicing emotions 1

This teacher is using his own emotions to model emotional literacy:

> What exactly is happening here?
> Why am I getting annoyed?

In this way, he makes the children aware of his annoyance and the cause. He is not criticising the children's behaviour; he is owning his own feelings, labelling them and making explicit a constructive way to deal with them. Through discussion, he helps the children understand that the way they all behave can have an impact on someone else's emotions.

Voicing emotions 2

The children are working in pairs on a maths problem, and the room is full of shouting and arguments.

Teacher: *Everybody stop. Stop and listen. Why do you think I have stopped you from your maths challenge?*

Child: *Because we were noisy.*

Teacher: *It wasn't so much the noise as what was making you noisy. What was that?*

Child: *Me and Sarah were arguing.*

Teacher: *It wasn't just you. It sounded like everyone in the room was arguing with their partner, and I was very worried that someone would get hurt. This is a priority right now. So put away your maths and come back to the carpet. We are going to sit down as a class, and we are going to speak about it now.*

In this way the teacher is making explicit that her worry is for the children or her worry about the consequences of the behaviour in the room. The teacher is also showing the children that relationships and social and emotional issues in the classroom are important and, in this instance, take priority over maths. The relationships and emotions within them are being valued. The teacher will then use this opportunity to develop further emotional literacy through relevant work on collaborative working, considering others or resolving differences, whichever is most relevant.

In this way, an emotionally literate teacher who embodies positive mental health is an essential component of the positive relationships at the heart of positive mental health promotion.

In this chapter social and emotional development is presented as a core component of positive mental health. Thus, emotional literacy development in schools is a fundamental part of positive mental health promotion. Emotional literacy is defined as incorporating the following capacities used for the benefit of others as well as self:

- self-understanding,
- recognizing and experiencing a range of emotions,
- understanding the causes and deciding how to act,
- understanding social situations,
- expressing emotions appropriately,
- recognizing emotions in others and experiencing empathy,
- developing relationships.

The importance of the teacher as a model of emotional literacy is emphasised. There are examples of ways in which elements of emotional literacy can be modelled and developed.

The chapter concludes with the audit questions for pupils and staff so that development needs and strengths can be identified.

Audit emotional literacy questions for pupils

Do the children in the classroom talk about how they feel? If so, please give an example.
Are you encouraged to talk about your feelings?
Does it feel safe to talk about feelings in your classroom?
What makes it feel safe/unsafe to talk about feelings?
Does your teacher talk about her/his feelings?
Does your teacher talk about the feelings of children in the class?
Does your teacher teach you about feelings?
Do you talk about the feelings of characters in fiction (stories/poems/films/TV)?
What do you do at school if you feel: (You might do different things.)

Angry?
Worried?
Happy?
Scared?
Jealous?
Excited?
Proud?
Embarrassed?
Sorry?
Miserable?

Audit emotional literacy questions for school staff

Do the children in the classroom talk about how they feel? If so, please give an example.
Are children encouraged to talk about their feelings?
What do you do to make children feel safe talking about their feelings?
Do you ever talk about your feelings? Give an example or say why if you do not.
Do you talk about the feelings of the children in the class?
What direct teaching of emotional literacy do you do?
Are you emotionally literate?
Do you model emotional literacy? Give an example.
Would you like more training or support with emotional literacy development?

6 Empowering children as learners

This chapter explains how ownership of learning contributes to wellbeing. Independence, realistic confidence and a sense of achievement all contribute to positive metal health. The chapter explores what is meant by ownership of learning. It suggests ways in which, through a focus on metacognition, teachers can help children understand how they learn best so they have greater ownership of their learning.

Dweck's (2017) texts on mindset, Hattie's (2012) on visible learning and my own book co-authored with Pete Tarrant (Tarrant and Holt, 2016) on metacognition all give practical guidance and some background rationale to the ways in which we can help children increase their awareness and understanding of their learning processes. In this chapter, I explore how this is an integral part of wellbeing promotion and take a closer look at how some specific characteristics can be promoted through empowering children as learners.

How ownership of learning contributes to wellbeing

Chapter 2 explores the relationship between positive mental health and learning. Empowerment can enhance wellbeing, and, in return, the promotion of mentally healthy characteristics such as self-confidence, resilience and self-esteem can increase motivation to learn, enjoyment of learning and academic achievement.

In this way, it is clear that wellbeing promotion through empowerment in learning is a fundamental part of being a teacher and not something that takes up additional time or conflicts with the core purpose of teaching. As one Scottish teacher explained:

> For me if my children don't understand themselves as learners, I feel that I may as well not be here.

Positive mental health promotion can be achieved through development and nurturing in the child of characteristics conducive to positive mental health. These characteristics should be developed through a broad range of experiences within the school. The process of making decisions about their learning and the activities they are engaging in strengthens the child's ability and confidence to make informed decisions.

A teacher is making a significant contribution to positive mental health promotion if they are helping the children in their class become better at assessing and establishing where they are with their learning. It is possible to increase pupils' confidence as learners through reflective practice in which pupils are guided to take responsibility for their own learning. There are even some claims that it is more important to a child's wellbeing to help them work out where they are with their learning than to reward them for making progress.

What is ownership of learning?

So what is meant here by empowerment? In the classroom, children empowered as learners will have the knowledge, skills and understanding to take ownership of their learning. This is a more complicated process than it might seem, and if ownership of learning is to promote wellbeing, it needs to be addressed carefully and in a planned way. Again I would refer the reader to *Metacognition in the Primary Classroom* (Tarrant and Holt, 2016) for a detailed guide to empowering children as learners. Here it is relevant to summarise the aims and main steps involved.

Children who are empowered as learners will be:

- aware of some of the ways that they learn,
- aware of some of the skills and tools that they use to learn,
- able to think and talk about what they learn and how they learn,
- able to discuss ways that they can work on being better at our learning.

For the teacher, this means:

- making the learning process explicit – the 'how' of learning, not just the 'what';
- embedding the language of learning into the classroom;
- giving pupils the skills with which to reflect on their learning;
- providing opportunities for meaningful reflection and self-evaluation;
- supporting pupils to work out how they can learn better.

Self- and peer evaluation as means of assessment are popular, not just because they seem like a time-efficient way to achieve formative assessment. However, within the busy classroom, with the time pressures that teachers face and the requirement to be accountable, evidence and product can suddenly be more important than process. Traffic lights and smiley faces are not enough; the children soon learn which colour or face to draw for an easy life or peer approval. If they don't get 'found out', their investment in or motivation for the process moves away from meaningful self-evaluation and can become a meaningless exercise that provides 'evidence' of assessment or attainment but does not leave the children feeling particularly good about themselves or any more aware of how they learn.

There is nothing wrong with simple systems for collecting and recording self- and peer assessment, but the process leading up to the recording needs to involve genuine reflection and consideration of learning if we want attainment to rise and children's confidence, self-esteem and general wellbeing to improve. Wellbeing is best promoted (and attainment raised) when a child is able to complete a challenging task, reflect on how they have achieved it, recognise the learning styles and skills that helped them and identify next steps for learning or ways they might do it differently next time.

Ways to empower children as learners

Positive mental health can be promoted through learner independence and achievement, and such independence requires skills, understanding and opportunities to experience challenge.

The first step is to build the language of learning. Ways that the teacher can do this include:

- making the language of learning explicit in teaching,
- introducing key language gradually,
- encouraging the children to identify and name ***how*** they are learning,
- embedding the language of learning into classroom life and the physical environment,
- having a focus on planning ***how*** the children will learn (target specific skills and the relevant language),
- building in opportunities to ***think*** and ***talk about*** the learning process.

It can be a valuable experience to get children to identify what a learner is, to ask:

> What makes a good learner?
> What skills and attitudes will a good learner have?

Part of the process of increasing self-confidence and resilience as learners can require a change in the concept or understanding of what learning or success entails as this teacher explains:

> The days are gone where a good learner is someone who sits still and puts their hand up. Today a good learner is someone who is resilient, resourceful and ready to learn, who is in a mindset to learn and an environment to learn.

Alongside such consideration of a learner's characteristics, reflection and self-evaluation skills should be developed. The teacher could:

a model reflection,
b give a template or structure for reflection,
c have specific lessons on reflecting and interview skills for learning conversations.

I will consider the first two points briefly here but refer the reader to other texts for a more comprehensive guide on developing reflective practice in the classroom.

a Model reflecting on something they have done. Something visual is a good start; for example, the teacher might draw a face and then reflect out loud on what looks right and how they achieved that:

What have I done well? I think I have the face shape right. It is not a regular circle; it is more oval and goes in at the chin.

What could be better? Let me think ... There is something not right about the eyes and nose. I think I need to look more closely at someone's face to see where the eyes and nose go.

The key skill emphasised here is looking closely or observation.

As teachers we regularly model the process of spelling, reading or writing in literacy lessons and problem solving or calculations in numeracy. When teaching children to reflect, we need to make explicit the process or learning skills used, not just the solution. In language, that might be talking about how we have to listen carefully to a word and keep trying different ways and strategies to help us spell. Reflective prompts might be:

- Am I using memory of how I have spelt a word before?
- Am I thinking carefully about the sound of the word?
- Am I drawing on previous learning and applying patterns and rules?
- Am I using other strategies such as mnemonics?

Such questions focus on how we are learning rather than the correct answer and so help the children become more aware of how they learn.

b Giving a template for reflection, such as the questions listed previously or something more visual, can help the children have a go at reflecting on their own. This might be working through a series of prompts, having a quick learning conversation with a partner or identifying the learning skills used from a list of learning words. At the end of a piece of work, the children might be taught how to reflect and then be given opportunities to reflect on:

  - How did I manage this?
  - How did I get here?
  - What was easy?
  - What was challenging?
  - What skills and strategies did I use today?
  - What could I work on to improve?
  - How might I transfer any of this learning?
  - Which skills do I need to work on?

c Specific lessons on reflection and interview skills for learning conversations.

If we want children to engage meaningfully in reflection, they will need to be taught how to reflect. The questions in this chapter make a useful framework or prompt. The focus needs to be thinking about how they learned, rather than what. Many of the strategies mentioned here are discussed in more detail in *Metacognition in the Primary Classroom* (Tarrant and Holt, 2016). For positive mental health promotion purposes, suffice to say that, for true ownership of learning and the health benefits that come from that, time will need to be spent giving the children the skills to reflect and engage in thinking and talking about how they learn.

What does effective empowerment look like?
Success criteria for the empowered learner

It is important for teachers and pupils to know what they are aiming for. Success criteria for an empowered learner are listed here:

- know what their strengths are and are able to identify their own next steps;
- talk about their own learning journey with understanding;
- are better at assessing and establishing where they are with their learning;
- are able to reflect after a lesson on what has been a success, how they learned and what helped them move forwards;
- help the teacher set the learning intentions and success criteria;
- can see whether they have achieved that success because they actually set the targets in the first place;
- are feeling more confident in their work.

Empowerment across all school life

There is a need to empower children holistically, in line with most effective positive mental health promotion. Any steps taken to value the child's voice and involve children in all aspects of school life can be seen as empowering.

Fundamental to this is the work undertaken to create an ethos for positive behaviour and learning. The children should be involved in discussing and agreeing together a class charter or code of conduct.

Empowering children also includes the solution circles mentioned in Chapter 7 and social development in which children are given the opportunity to make suggestions and help others deal with tricky situations. This leads into helping children develop the tools and skills to resolve their own problems and disputes independently.

Hornby and Atkinson (2003) believe the teacher has a responsibility to develop an ethos in which children, school staff and parents all have and understand their roles in positive mental health promotion. Reflective practice thrives in a supportive environment but also helps children develop the skills and characteristics desirable to a supportive environment. The sense of ownership and connectedness to school is enhanced by procedures that empower children, such as giving them the skills and opportunities to contribute to the whole school community and giving them a voice in school decisions (Hall, 2010). In turn, such pupil investment and the greater sense of connectedness they feel to school has benefits for their positive mental health.

> If you can create a culture where you can discuss things and reflect on things that have happened, then you are building the children up to be reflective people to reflect on their actions and change them if need be or to do things for themselves.

It is important to involve children in the work to promote positive mental health. Strategies and initiatives such as those discussed will help the children learn about positive mental health and how to promote it so that they are better able to make informed decisions and evaluations of their own lives and classes. For example, children may learn about resilience within a specific lesson, and they can then use this knowledge to work as a class to find ways to become more resilient or help others do so. The pupil responses to the audit questions at the end of this chapter are intended to be considered along with those of school staff to get the best perspective of the contributors and barriers to positive mental health in the school. They will help identify the desire, skills and development needs of children and staff and the ways in which these can be used and addressed to draw up a whole-school positive mental health plan - one that has the ownership and understanding of both the children and the adults in the school. A survey of just the pupils or just the school staff, whilst informative, does not give the whole picture and does not show any potential difference in perspective.

Practical approaches

The practical approaches outlined next will work best within an ethos of positive mental health promotion. Many aspects relate directly to suggestions and strategies offered in Chapter 4.

Confidence, self-esteem and sense of achievement

When developing an ethos in which it is OK to get it wrong, as discussed in Chapter 4, it can be helpful to reconsider class approaches to ability grouping and differentiation. As teachers, we constantly and routinely evaluate and assess a child's achievements and development needs so that we can plan for appropriate next steps in learning. A few questions to consider:

1 How does teacher-formative assessment fit in with encouraging children to have ownership of their own learning?
2 How does this sit alongside self- and peer evaluation?

How this works will vary according to individual need and the age groups taught. Each teacher will have to find the balance that works best for the children in their class every year. What is important is that teachers are not giving mixed messages.

3 Are we telling children to self-evaluate but then overruling this with our evaluation and ability grouping or differentiated task?
4 If so, why?
5 Where is their self-evaluation going wrong?
6 Have we given them sufficient understanding of how to reflect?
7 Have the children and teacher a shared understanding of the learning outcomes and success criteria or, in other words, what they are learning and what it will look like if it is achieved?

Teachers recognise that a lack of confidence often causes children to put limits on their own learning and that ability grouping sometimes reinforces children's negative self-concepts.

There are many possible strategies to overcome this. It can be helpful to take an approach such as the currently popular chilli approach, in which children are given a choice of activities that they can choose in order to achieve their next steps in learning. Instead of placing children in ability or mixed-ability groups, such an approach involves providing opportunities for children to select for themselves the difficulty level of the task. If this is to be a successful way of increasing confidence and sense of achievement, it does need to take place within a supportive ethos, a classroom in which children are supported to value, respect and encourage each other. The aim is to build confidence and for pupils to achieve their learning potential. They have to feel able to choose what they think is appropriate for them, rather than feeling that they have to do what their friend does or feeling pressure to take an option that is too easy or too hard.

Using self-selection as a way to empower children as learners will be most effective within the kind of ethos described in Chapter 4 and with the positive relationships and emotional literacy skills discussed in Chapters 3 and 5. The concept of self-selection needs to be introduced with explicit reference to relevant aspects of the ethos and levels of behaviour towards others that are expected. Alongside this, it is useful to start with a discussion of why children go to school. The beliefs and understandings children have in answer to this question can be a helpful starting point for all work on learning and empowerment as learners. Bearing in mind that, for many children, school is a place to meet friends and socialise, it can also be useful to consider the question of what school can do for us and how school will learning be useful.

After such discussions, there should be sufficient shared understanding to explore scenarios in which a child might choose a too easy/too challenging piece of work. Throughout the scenarios and discussions, the teacher needs to model the nonjudgemental attitude expected from the children and essential to the success of the approach.

Scenarios: Why take the easy one?

Kirstine was scared of science because her dad and brothers said it was a man's subject, and girls were too silly. Kirstine enjoyed the early work on making circuits so that lights lit up, but when she was given three science tasks on electricity from which to choose, she picked the easy one because she believed that girls could only do the easy tasks.

Niki had gone through school so far finding everything easy, but the recent science topic of electricity was quite tricky as she was not used to making decisions and trying different ways. She decided that she would pick the easy science task because she wanted to feel good about her work. She would hate to get something wrong.

Josh found school boring. He loved science and read books about it all the time at home. He decided he was going to do all the science tasks, starting with the easy one, just so he could do extra science and not be so bored.

Simon found electricity really hard. He was a bit confused by all the words used, and he was not sure he understood what they had done so far. He chose the easy task.

Archie chose the difficult task last time, and it was too hard, so he was not going to do that again. It was horrible to have to try again.

Karen thought she could probably do the medium task, but as it had been a week since they did electricity, she thought that it would be a good idea to do the easy one first to get her back into science.

- These are all common reasons for choosing an easy task, but are they the right choice for these children?
- Will the easy task challenge each child and help them to move forwards in their learning?
- If another task would be more suitable, which one and why?

Ask the children to consider these scenarios and then use them to discuss issues arising:

- Do we let someone else's opinion cloud our own judgement?
- Are we influenced by other people in ways that stop our learning?
- Should everything be so easy that we get nothing wrong?
- Where is the learning if we don't ever find anything difficult?
- Does getting something wrong mean there is something wrong with us?
- Should we get everything right easily all the time?
- Is there any shame in doing an easy task?
- How do we find out new things or what we need to learn?

One teacher explains:

> I was talking about mistakes being OK in my maths lesson the other day. It was really difficult getting the children to the idea that actually getting it all right is not necessarily success, and maybe I had pitched the lesson wrong if they got everything right all the time. I explained that if they were starting to get things wrong, that meant it was challenging, and that is a good thing. I feel like I have got a lot of work to do with them in that respect.

It is good for the children to see that there are many reasons for the choices others make when selecting a difficulty level. Discussions such as these should help remove any stigma associated with doing the easy task or choosing a harder one and getting something wrong. These messages need to be reinforced through the expectations and responses given in class during such self-selected activities. In this way, children begin to have the self-awareness, understanding of learning and confidence to choose appropriately. They experience challenge and success as well as developing academic resilience.

The aim is to work towards a class climate in which children are not afraid of challenge and can see mistakes as a constructive part of the learning process rather than the end of the world and something to be avoided at all costs. Sometimes, when we remove ceilings in this way, children exceed our expectations as teachers and perhaps their own.

For confidence and a real sense of achievement, the culture in the classroom is crucial. Some ways this is reinforced and the benefits are illustrated in the comments of these teachers:

> We need the children to embrace the idea and support each other with the idea that making mistakes is OK.
>
> I always say to my class, 'It's OK to be wrong because that will then help me to teach you, to make you better.'

> There's no such thing as a failure; it's an opportunity to learn something. We have been a lot more conscious as professionals of the language that we use and how we instil that in the children.
>
> I see a huge difference in the children because they are not scared to get things wrong. It's all right to get things wrong. That seems to be a huge pressure lifted.

Independence and pupil-led learning

As children begin to understand themselves as learners, it can be much better for their growing independence and sense of achievement if, when they identify areas of difficulty, channels of support are available for them. Some schools accompany self-evaluation with a self-referral process where children can refer themselves for additional support in an area that they find challenging or in which they have been making slow progress. This situates the child as an active player in their own learning; they are asking for support or advice to get to their next stage in learning. This might be direct support from a teacher or teaching assistant, or it might be in the form of signposting to useful websites or tasks that will help them address the issues raised. It should be seen as something everyone can do and not as the last resort of the desperate!

As the children begin to understand how they learn, they will become more aware of the things that influence their learning, such as their feelings about a subject. As part of their development, they may choose to build their confidence in maths or use what they enjoy about one subject to help them in another.

The importance of transferable skills cannot be overstated. Children who understand how they are learning and their strengths in learning are better able to transfer their skills. Take, for example, the child who dislikes maths and loves PE. In reflecting on their PE, they may identify that they are good at persevering or good at trying different ways to solve a problem. These are skills also required in maths. Knowing that they have some relevant skills to bring to their maths work can increase confidence and self-belief.

Every child will identify a strength that they can, with support and guidance, bring to an area where they have fewer strengths. Take the example of the child who loved to draw, could reproduce images and create cartoons and made excellent use of colour. She carried around the belief that all she could do was draw and that she was no good at anything else. Teachers praised her drawing to raise her confidence, but this only served to make her aware of the more frequent times when she was not praised in subjects that seemed to be valued more highly by the school, such as maths and writing. By reflecting on the learning processes and skills involved in drawing, the child was able to identify some of the things that made her good at drawing: concentration, careful observation, good spatial awareness, perseverance. Reflection and self-evaluation in maths and writing made her aware that all the skills and attitudes that made her so good at drawing were transferable to other subjects. Identifying ways in which observation and spatial awareness were needed in maths gave her the confidence to tackle tasks that helped her develop other maths skills. It is not a magic cure, but children's understanding of their transferable skills can begin to bring down barriers, reducing fear and increasing motivation and achievement in other areas.

Another way to promote ownership of learning and positive mental health is for the children to use their self-evaluation and reflective skills in contributing to their personal portfolios or learning journals. The children will be able to identify new challenges and achievements and suggest ways to include these in a personal achievement file. They are again working in partnership with teachers on assessment and evaluation, rather than being reported on.

It works best if children have frequent access to their personal portfolios so that they become like scrapbooks of their achievements through the year. They can choose when to add something and explain why. If portfolios are readily available, the children can also just enjoy looking through them, celebrating achievements and reflecting on the things of which they are proud. It is something that children can share meaningfully with a visitor or parent on parents' evening because they have ownership of it.

This increases ownership and promotes positive mental health in many ways:

- It serves as a concrete reminder of who the children are and their achievements, particularly important for children whose home lives are inconsistent or changing.
- It increases engagement in the learning process so that children can play an active role in setting learning intentions and success criteria.
- As the children look back at what they have achieved, it can boost their confidence and remind them of what is possible.

In summary, this chapter has:

- explained how empowering children as learners contributes to positive mental health;
- defined ownership of learning as a child being aware of some of the ways that they learn and able to think and talk about what they learn, how they learn and how they can become better at their learning;
- clarified the links between empowerment and other approaches to wellbeing promotion;
- presented ways to increase ownership of learning and empower children as learners.

Audit questions for school staff – empowering children as learners

Do you provide opportunities for children to reflect on their learning? Give examples.
Do you help children develop the skills they need to reflect meaningfully on their learning? If so give examples; if not, say why.
What steps do you take to empower children as learners/help them engage meaningfully in self-evaluation and target setting?
Are these successful?
How could these be more successful?

Audit questions for pupils – empowering children as learners

Do you have time to think about how your learning is going?

Do you know how to reflect on a task you have done?

Do you know how you learn?

Thinking of **how** you work, not **what** you do, please answer the following:

What kinds of learning do you find easy?

What kinds of learning do you find difficult?

How do you know when you have done well?

What do you do when you find something difficult?

Do you know what your next steps in learning are in any subject?

Can you talk about your strengths and development needs?

What do you do when you have achieved a development need?

7 Embedded promotion and targeted action

This chapter explores the role of commercial, evidence-based and national strategies and the symbiotic relationship between embedded approaches and discrete lessons. It acknowledges the value of using commercial or national schemes and resources for discrete lessons whilst explaining how to make sure that they are used most effectively. The key to success is knowing which approaches to use and when. The chapter should be read alongside Chapters 3 to 6.

Commercial and national strategies

There are already a range of commercial schemes, national curriculum guidance and wellbeing promotion resources that help build a child's positive mental health. There is plenty of research and evaluation of such strategies to show that, whether targeted at specific children or used universally with all pupils, such schemes and strategies do help remove barriers to positive mental health and help nurture healthy development.

As argued in the previous chapters, such targeted development of mentally healthy skills and capacities can be essential to a child's ability to contribute to a supportive ethos, take ownership of learning or engage in a positive relationship. A review of the most effective approaches to positive mental health promotion, such as those discussed in Chapter 2, would conclude that, for most successful positive mental health promotion, a combination of strategies and universal approaches is required. This chapter looks briefly at what this might mean in the classroom.

Making connections

Teachers often explore set social or emotional themes in specific PSHE or health and wellbeing lessons. This can be part of a whole-school scheme such as Creating Confident Kids in Scotland or the previously recommended Social and Emotional Aspects of Learning in England and Wales. Or it might be through use of resources from a commercial scheme such as Emotion Works. As evaluations reveal, sometimes curriculum pressures and time constraints mean that only the core lesson is actually addressed, and then only occasionally, meaning that positive mental health promotion is much less likely to be successful. It seems that health education is often the first thing to be missed out when the pressure to attain a desired standard and to achieve in core areas such as literacy and numeracy dominate. Unfortunately, when such themes as friendship or bullying are restricted to curriculum activities as a learning experience, abstract from the social experience of the classroom, the children do not always see their relevance to real life. The learning becomes cognitive, something they know and can talk about in the same way they might talk about magnets or Vikings. However, what they need is for the learning to be personal, something that informs the way they act and live. So how can this be achieved?

A core part of any wellbeing approach is to help children see the connection to their lives within and outside the classroom. The themes and learning from specific schemes should be reinforced throughout the school day at the most relevant times. For example, if children fall out during a group task, the teacher should ask them to remember what they have learned about working with others or how to resolve conflict instead of stepping in to sort out the problem. Alternatively, it might be appropriate to draw on their emotional literacy work and ask children to think about how another child may be feeling or about how the way they are behaving is influenced by their feelings. Having social and emotional success criteria in addition to the wider curriculum learning intentions can also help children see the relevance of a health and wellbeing lesson to their daily classroom life.

It is also useful to remind children that, all through their lives, they are likely to encounter conflicts to resolve and new relationships to be built or repaired. Using the real-life experiences of the adults in the school or drawing attention to them when they occur in fiction can be a way to help children see that they are developing lifelong skills. When I was in the classroom, I often heard children say in response to a range of curriculum areas and social skills: 'I don't need to know this. I am going to drive a skip lorry when I grow up' or some other future life intention. It can be quite useful to get insight into what the children think they will do later in their lives as the teacher can then identify and help the child see the social and emotional skills and attitudes that they will need to draw on in this future life. This helps the children see the relevance of the social and emotional learning to their lives and can provide motivation for them to develop specific skills.

This links to the empowerment of children discussed in Chapters 3 and 6. The classroom becomes seen as a place for the acquisition of lifelong skills. Teachers need to move away from being perceived as problem fixers to being someone who facilitates the children's own problem solving and who provides resources or prompts that help the children manage this independently. There is a wealth of such capacity-building resources available. Ideally, any prompts or scaffolding to help the children become more independent in dealing with social and emotional situations should be available in the classroom all the time, either on display or as cards or prompt sheets to be accessed as needed. The work in discrete lessons should be reinforced constantly through the class and school behaviour codes. The teacher should be a positive role model for the healthy capacities and social behaviours, and positive reinforcement for such ways of being should be embedded into classroom life.

Solution circles

One way in which to make meaningful connections between specific social and emotional learning and life is to hold regular solution circles. In order for any class listen-and-respond activity to be successful, the children first need to be experienced in the format. Jenny Moseley's Circle Time resources can help build a child's understanding of the skills and ethos required for circle time sharing. Before children can engage in a solution circle, work will need to be done on listening, what it is to be a listener and how to respond respectfully and with empathy. (See Chapters 3 to 6 for more details.) Rules need to be negotiated and agreed. Solution circles depend on some level of positive relationships, a safe and supportive ethos and early emotional awareness. Consistent with healthy social and emotional development, the children need a level of development in order to engage in social and emotional activities, and through this engagement, their social and emotional development will increase further.

In some circles, the children speak in turn as a speaking object such as a spoon or teddy is passed around; in others they put up their hand to request the object, or it is passed from one speaker to another determined by the last speaker. Children may always pass on the object without speaking, but everyone should be encouraged to contribute and to be aware that their contribution will be valued and respected.

First solution circles might be ones in which the teacher brings a scenario to the class and encourages the children to think of:

- how they would feel in that situation and what they might need,
- what they might do or say to the person in that situation.

The children are encouraged to contribute to the circle with their thoughts, ideas or responses to the situation. They are then asked to think of a solution. What do they suggest the person with the problem do next?

Once solution circles are established, they can be embedded into classroom routines. They should take place weekly or even more often if possible. The focus can be child led or chosen by the teacher to address a specific need or to reinforce the teaching in specific health and wellbeing lessons. There might be a worry box or 'ask the group' box prominently placed in the classroom in which children can place their own problems or fears for consideration in the solution circle. Problems can go to the circle anonymously or named. When combined with specific wellbeing teaching and embedded within a supportive ethos, solution circles can be an effective way to help children see the real-life meaning of their learning whilst also developing healthy characteristics such as resilience, emotional literacy, consideration for others and conflict resolution, to name but a few. As the quote from this newly qualified teacher explains:

> One of the new pupils shared about having no one to play with in Circle Time and how it made him feel. Everybody else in the class was a bit upset. They talked about how they could make sure everyone is included in the playground. Now they all come in from playtime and tell me how they made sure that all the class were all right and had someone to play with.

In this way, a daily or weekly routine such as solution circles can be used to help reinforce the learning from specific health and wellbeing lessons. Children become better able to see that what they learned is about being and living and can help them in the classroom and their lives outside school.

In summary, specific teaching for positive mental health promotion is most effective when this teaching is reinforced and modelled through embedded approaches such as class and school ethos and positive relationships. Having a 'bridge' such as a solution circles activity that helps children see the connections can be one way to do this. As previously mentioned, the importance of the teacher as positive role model is also essential.

Something to think about

Positive mental health promotion may include discrete lessons on a range of capacities or issues, such as:

- specific emotions:
  - fear,
  - jealousy,
  - happiness,
  - enthusiasm,
  - pride,
  - sadness;
- making friends,
- resolving arguments and friendship problems,
- bullying,
- valuing self,
- looking after self (personal safety),
- resilience,
- grief and loss,
- positive mindset,
- peer pressure,
- sex education.

The list goes on. Sometimes the theme is chosen because it is meeting a need that has been identified during normal classroom life (for example, mindset or resilience). At other times, the health-promoting curriculum or scheme might dictate the timing or topic of the lesson. In such cases, when planning the lesson, it is helpful to:

- Identify all the times in the school day, week or year when such a characteristic is likely to occur.
- Plan ways in which to make explicit the connections between the learning and school life.
- Plan how the focus will be reinforced and praised during the whole day (outside the discrete lesson).
- Identify links between the theme and the school vision or school policies.

- Consider who else in the school will be with a child when they may experience this, such as lunchtime staff, PE specialists etc. and find ways to share plans and rationales with them.
- Consider links to home life and ways to include parents within the theme.

Once these steps have been carried out, the teacher will be in a much stronger position to embed the health promotion learning into everyday life, making it more meaningful and strengthening the children's understanding and capacity to develop. (See Appendix 20.)

Resources for positive mental health promotion - barriers and facilitators

As with positive mental health promotion generally, a lack of resources or the frequent requirement to implement different strategies is a recognised challenge to the teacher's role in positive mental health promotion.

Commercial schemes and national resources such as Restorative Practice or Creating Confident Kids are seen by teachers as good ways for them to increase their skills in elements of health promotion and as sources of resources to use with the children. However, training, commitment and a continued whole-school valuing of the initiative are required for the full benefits to be realised. Even when nominally part of a whole-school policy, some initiatives are not always effective as ways to promote positive mental health because of a lack of time or resources:

- Everyone using the approach or resource needs to know what they are doing and why, how it promotes positive mental health.
- Every class has to have sufficient resources and be using them appropriately.
- Resources cannot be shared by classes or rotated around the school if a whole-school approach is expected. Issues need to be addressed as they are relevant in the classroom, not only when it is the class's turn to use the resource.
- Staff need dedicated time to work with new schemes and resources so that they become confident enough to embed elements into their daily practice.
- Staff need time to talk to each other about the approach, to share problems and good ideas.
- Professional learning related to a resource is essential, but it is not enough on its own. Teachers also need time and support to embed what they have learned.
- The resource or approach needs to remain high profile if it is to be embedded and used all the time.

Schemes and resources have the potential to enhance school positive mental health promotion, but limitations, such as availability of resources and time to learn how best to employ them, can contribute to the demands and frustrations of positive mental health promotion.

In summary, this chapter has discussed the value of schemes and resources to positive mental health promotion. There are a range of useful commercial and freely available resources that will help teachers develop specific elements of positive mental health within a wider whole-school approach. This chapter suggests ways to embed them and maximise their potential and has acknowledged some of the challenges to success.

Part III

Strategies for developing whole-school positive mental health promotion

8 The importance of a whole-school approach

Mental health promotion is context specific, so after presenting a case for a whole-school approach, this chapter offers suggestions and frameworks for whole-school professional learning (INSET) to develop a positive mental health promotion strategy that meets the needs of a school. The audit in the Appendix, which involves the questions presented at the end of each related chapter, forms the starting point for any whole-school approach.

The chapter also includes opportunities to explore the existing understanding of and attitudes towards positive mental health of staff within the school and find out the hopes and fears of teachers in relation to positive mental health and their role in promotion.

Whole-school organisation

In Chapter 2, the key elements of successful promotion were presented. Factors relating to whole-school coordination, communication and collaboration dominate. A review of the research and evaluations of mental health promotion reveals agreement that rather than random short-term interventions, positive mental health promotion in schools requires a planned approach incorporating long-term strategies and coordinated whole-school policies. These should be designed to increase health-promoting elements and reduce factors likely to demote positive mental health (Bielsa et al., 2010; Green et al., 2005; Cushman, Clelland and Hornby, 2011).

My own recent research concludes that teachers recognise that a holistic approach in which the child is immersed in consistent messages and behaviours conducive to positive mental health cannot be done by an individual alone. It has to be part of a whole-school philosophy, part of a lived experience, not just a conceptual plan. The school and all within it need to embody positive mental health promotion. It is not enough for the school to have positive mental health promotion as one of many actions on the school improvement plan. The teacher's work in the classroom needs to be endorsed and reinforced by practice elsewhere in the school.

Every member of the school community needs to have a role in positive mental health promotion. Teachers working to promote wellbeing agree that it is easier to do so when there is a whole-school focus providing a professional learning community in which teachers and staff can support each other to find the best ways to implement and develop further promotion approaches. Research reveals that teachers as well as pupils benefit from being part of a whole school community where there are consistent policies and where they work in a nonjudgemental, health-promoting environment as this quote from a teacher illustrates:

> No matter how committed a professional you are, you need to be in an environment where it is a team effort, where everybody is believing in it and investing in it.

It is important that promotion programmes and long-term strategies are consistent with the school's ethos and vision and that they have the support of all involved. This requires careful planning informed by the culture of the school and the needs of both individuals and the whole school community.

Compatible school culture is essential. Teachers working in schools that value or prioritise positive mental health promotion do not experience the same level of conflict between the pressure to progress pupil learning and the responsibility to promote positive mental health.

School leadership

Whatever the level of change required in the introduction or development of a school's positive mental health promoting practice, the school leadership have an important role. Unless school leaders ensure or undertake effective coordination, monitoring, ongoing development and improvement of a planned programme of positive mental health promotion, there is minimal impact on the pupils, and it becomes unsustainable (Ekornes, Hauge and Lund, 2012; Greenberg et al., 2003). School leaders who understand positive mental health promotion are better able to motivate and inspire school staff. In the words of Herrman, Saxena and Moodie (2005), someone at a high level in the school has to 'champion' the programme. School leaders are instrumental in reducing or removing barriers to promotion through ensuring sufficient time, resources and training (Han and Weiss, 2005). Without the support of school leadership, staff development tends to be insufficient, and staff are less likely to commit to promotion.

According to research and evaluation of practice, school leaders knowledgeable in positive mental health promotion are better able to inspire and motivate staff to engage effectively in promotion initiatives (Hallam, 2009; Han and Weiss, 2005; Herrman, Saxena and Moodie, 2005). As you might expect, in contrast, conflicting practices across a school, inconsistent messages and the absence of a shared school vision or a shared understanding of positive mental health promotion are barriers to promotion and contributors to poor mental health in teachers and pupils (Gu and Day, 2007; Kelchtermans, 2011; Mayer, 2011; Milkie and Warner, 2011).

Positive mental health promotion in a school does not have to be led by the headteacher, particularly if another senior colleague has relevant experience, understanding and commitment. Effective positive mental health promotion in many schools is overseen by the deputy or a senior teacher in collaboration with the head. The dialogue and planning that comes from two professionals coming together with slightly different priorities – for example, evidencing attainment versus pupil wellbeing – can lead to stronger, more effective plans and strategies. There needs to be discussion and a level of healthy debate to effect true change.

Audit next steps – parents

Have parents been included?

It may be appropriate to issue surveys to parents. Alternatively, it might be more useful to have parents' meetings where promotion strategies are discussed and parental perspectives on the needs of their children are gathered. Another way to involve parents is to ask pupils to devise questions and collect information from their parents under the key headers of the audit.

- What are their perspectives on the priorities for positive mental health promotion?
- What are parents' fears in relation to their child's mental health?
- What do parents think the school does well to promote positive mental health?

Audit response for leaders of wellbeing promotion

Once the audit or each part of the audit has been carried out, there are tasks for those leading positive mental health promotion to identify priorities for development, training needs and next steps. It is expected that development in relation to each aspect of the review can be informed by the relevant chapters in this book. (See Appendices 12 and 13.)

Questions to consider

- What are the barriers to positive mental health promotion identified in the audit?
- What do staff find to be working well?
- What do pupils identify as factors that make them feel good about school?
- Do staff and pupil opinions concur?
- If not, here is a priority starting point: find out more about the children's perspective and the staff to explore how and why there are differences.
- If they do agree, clear shared priorities should emerge.

Identify three agreed things about the school that are facilitating positive mental health promotion:

- Why are these working well?
- What strengths or characteristics are leading to this?
- How can these strengths and characteristics be used to support development in other areas?

Identify three priorities for change.

This is best done with groups of staff and pupils, but those leading the promotion would benefit from having some thoughts and plans ahead of the group discussions and planning.

Pick one or two priorities that will be quick to achieve and one that may take longer and need more development time and support. Is there one element of the audit in particular that stands out as a priority: for example, emotional literacy or ethos? If so, target the general theme.

If priorities seem to be spread out across different audit themes, then choose some that might be addressed together: for example, social skills and teacher as model.

Once priorities are identified, draw up a needs audit and action plan:

- What are the issues identified?
- How does practice differ from desired positive mental health promotion practice?
- Do staff need help building relevant knowledge?
- Do staff need help increasing their skills?
- What else is needed to begin to address the priority area?
- Are there any resources that would support the process: for example, Restorative Practice or Emotional Literacy packages?

Strategies and professional learning activities for a whole-school approach

(See Appendices 14–21.)

1 Mental health understanding part 1 – discussion activity for school staff

Small group activity: The audit asks the following questions.

Discuss your own answers with colleagues, exploring any differences and the potential reasons for these:

a) Do you have a secure understanding of positive mental health?
b) How would you define it?
c) What might a child with positive mental health be like?
d) What might a child with poor mental health be like?

Follow up as a whole group

a) Explore confidence levels. What level of understanding of positive mental health is there? There are so many misconceptions around that it is understandable to feel uncertain or to lack confidence in the concept of positive mental health. For those staff who wish to increase their understanding of positive mental health, Chapter 1 of this book is recommended reading. It also signposts you to further readings if required.
b) Shared understanding. Gather the various perspectives of positive mental health and try to come to an agreed, whole-school definition of what positive mental health is.
c) Shared understanding. In the same way, now collect characteristics of a child with positive mental health. Can these be represented pictorially? This is also an activity that can be carried out with children.

Figure 8.1 Positive mental health

d) Shared understanding. What are the many and varying characteristics of a child with poor mental health? Now think of the school itself. What kinds of mental health difficulties are present? What challenges to the children's mental health do they experience in their lives? Is there anything that leaps out as a priority for targeted strategies?

Additional small-group task: Ask small groups to talk about the stigma associated with mental health. Is there a fear of the term? Is the word 'mental' used as an insult or deficit adjective in the school? Do any colleagues believe that mental health is not part of their remit?

Additional whole-group follow-up: What challenges might we face in this school in relation to understanding mental health, community understanding and valuing of the terms and concept of positive mental health promotion? Do any immediately necessary actions become apparent?

Remember, positive mental health promotion is for all children, but some children might have particular challenges or be at risk of specific threats to mental health. Such children will benefit from the whole-school positive mental health promotion approaches, but effective promotion also includes removing risks to mental health, and this sometimes involves targeted strategies or specific small-group teaching in addition to the whole-school approaches. This is not to be confused with specific support for poor mental health, which may be offered by mental health specialists.

By the end of this first session, there should be agreement on the school definition of positive mental health promotion, what a child with positive mental health might look like and identification of threats and risks to mental health experienced by children in the school. It may feel like you have done nothing but talk. However, coming to a shared understanding and exploring attitudes, fears and perspectives is a crucial foundation for whole-school consistency.

2 Mental health understanding part 2 - discussion activity for school staff

Small-group activity: The audit asks the following questions. Discuss your own answers with colleagues, exploring any differences and the potential reasons for these:

a Do you teach children about emotional health or mental health?
b What kinds of things do you do?
c What explicit teaching do you do related to promoting the many elements of positive mental health promotion?
d What embedded practice do you have in place to promote positive mental health?

In this session, the aim is to get mixed groups of school staff to talk about what they already do and to tease out their understanding of embedded versus discrete positive mental health promotion.

Gather perspectives from the individual group discussions with the whole room and then give groups a scenario to discuss:

Scenario 1

The children in Alison's class are eight years old. They cannot work together without arguments. Alison has plans for group science activities and paired writing, but the children spend their time arguing, and the science or writing does not get done. Alison does not want a silent classroom where children work alone, so she decides to take time out from other lessons each day to work on collaboration.

She starts with lessons on what makes a good friend, how to work with a partner and what to do if there is a disagreement. She tries these lessons for a week and then returns to her plans for collaborative study.

What embedded wellbeing promotion needs to be in place for the targeted lessons on collaboration and friendship to move from conceptual to lived?

How does she support the children to move from talking about a good partner or friend to actually being one?

Scenario 2

Rob has a class of ten-year-olds. Whenever he gives them open-ended tasks or activities designed to challenge their thinking and problem solving, they end up lining up by his desk asking for help because they are frightened to get it wrong. They miss the security of a set method leading to a right answer.

Rob has read a lot on mindset and decides to introduce some specific sessions on mindset, daring to try and learning from mistakes.

What does he need to do to embed and reinforce these messages into his daily practice?

Discussion

There are no correct answers to this as every classroom and school will be different, but what we are working towards is a greater understanding of how what the teacher does all day every day reinforces and models the specific areas of social, emotional and mental wellbeing targeted in the discrete lessons.

Key messages we hope to come from the discussions are:

- growing understanding of the need for more than just a set of discrete lessons;
- teacher as model;
- consistent expectation;
- praise when children enact and embody the healthy characteristics sought (good friendship, conflict resolution etc.);
- support, examples and reminders of (for example) positive behaviour or positive attitude around the room to help children;
- avoidance of mixed messages - do not tolerate the undesired characteristics; instead use positive reinforcement.

3 Assessing social wellbeing - professional learning task

Discuss in groups:

- What skills, behaviours and attitudes would you expect a child to display?
- Target specific elements of social wellbeing.
- Draw up success criteria (SC) (as class/group and individual).
- Teach children how to evaluate self and others according to the target SC.
- Teach them how to give and receive feedback. (This is a social skill to develop a social skill.)

Share discussions in the whole room, then each group should carry out the next task using the image as a framework. (For contexts, see Appendix 16).

- Try it now - develop social SC for group activity.
- You will have your core subject SC; what social skills are necessary to the task?
- How will you know a child has demonstrated these skills?
- How will they be evaluated?
- What constructive feedback could be used?

Use the image in Figure 8.2 as a framework for devising your SC.

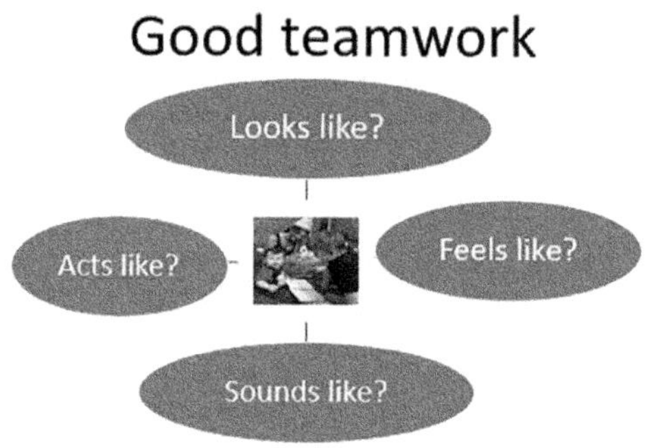

Figure 8.2 Good teamwork

Staff professional learning activity on ethos for positive mental health

One of the key reasons why a whole-school approach to positive mental health promotion is so important is the need for a consistent ethos. Without a supportive whole-school ethos, positive mental health promotion is significantly inhibited. The following professional learning activities could be used to follow engagement with the positive mental health audit.

4 Unpicking ethos – whole-school professional learning task

This might be a useful way to move forwards with a health-promoting ethos if that is the area of promotion identified as a development priority.

Group task 1

Give each group one of the following aspects of ethos:

- safe,
- respecting,
- supportive,
- inclusive.

Ask each group to consider what they do to make the school feel like the characteristic they have been given.

Collect three key actions or policies per group.
Now look at the pupil responses to the questions about ethos.
How does what the staff has identified match what the children say?
Discuss: do groups want to change their key actions in line with pupil responses?
Does everyone have and understand their roles in positive mental health promotion?

Group task 2

Each group has a different characteristic. Look at the pupil responses on what makes the school feel not such a good place to be:

- sense of belonging,
- acceptance,
- encouraging and rewarding positive behaviour,
- encouraging and praising positive social interaction,

Each group should discuss the priorities for change and the positives on which to build in relation to their characteristic.

Do any next steps or development needs stand out?

In between tasks 2 and 3, it would be helpful for those attending the professional learning sessions to have a day or a week to be thinking specifically about ethos as they carry out their daily work in school and as they move through different parts of the school. Each member of staff could be responsible for concentrating on a specific element to observe and gather more information. Individual practitioner enquiry tasks could bring valuable insight and understanding to the positive mental health promotion development process.

Group task 3

Look at the remaining characteristics of a health-promoting environment and evaluate where they think each class or the whole school does well or could do better:

- prohibiting discrimination and promoting equality;
- fostering positive relationships between staff, pupils and families;
- engendering in children a sense of security and achievement;
- encouraging and rewarding healthy behaviours in addition to academic achievement;
- praise and positive feedback;
- having emotionally literate teachers;
- giving children a valued voice in school decisions;
- empowering children;
- providing social and emotional support for those within the school;
- ensuring the school is physically in good repair with fit-for-purpose fittings and furniture.

Now consider the following questions:

What are the strengths of different parts of the school and the school as a whole?
Are there any school priorities?
How do children feel about being in the school?
What friendships and relationships do the children like?
What social elements do the children dislike?
Is there consistency across the children's responses?

If not, where are the differences? Is there any pattern? How can we find out why there are differences?
How do we feel to work here? What is it like to be here?
In this school, what do we want it to feel like to be a pupil and a teacher?
How can we achieve this?
How do we gather pupil perspective on this?

Use the discussion and teacher and pupil responses to draw up a plan for next steps or a whole-school health-promoting ethos development plan.

5 Planning whole-school positive mental health promotion

It may be that sessions need to be spread out to allow time to work with groups of children or to gauge opinion and pupil response to suggestions and plans.

Having looked at specific elements of the audit, it is useful now to consider staff and pupil responses across the whole audit in relation to the existing school vision and aims.

Discuss vision and aims:

1 What are the whole-school vision and aims?
2 What healthy characteristics promote this vision?
3 Are any aspects of this vision likely to demote positive mental health?

With the responses to these three questions about vision and aims in mind, look at all the responses from pupils and the perspectives of school staff and carry out next task.

Look at the key elements of successful positive mental health promotion below:

- consistent message,
- lived experience,
- relationship expectations,
- collective focus (e.g. on resilience or I can),
- endorsing and reinforcing what happens in the classroom throughout the school,
- shared language.

Come to a shared agreement on:

- what these elements should look like in this school,
- how they might be achieved,
- any staff development needs,
- any staff support or wellbeing needs,
- any specific child mental health promotion needs or risks that have to be addressed for successful positive mental health promotion,
- how to work with the whole community,
- identifying the support (if any) needed from outside agencies.

Identify what should be in the consistent health-promoting messages permeating the school.

Concluding comments

The aim of any professional learning or whole-staff work on positive mental health promotion should be to get a good understanding of the school context, strengths and needs; to identify priorities and to work out ways to achieve them. This should inform a whole-school plan which has a realistic timescale for introducing change, gathering opinion and evaluating progress. Change takes time. An approach might be effective and successful without showing any evidence of this for a good six months. It is important to give plans and changes time to embed and for approaches to be in place long enough to begin to have impact. Build in dates to take stock and review how it is going with pupils, staff and parents. Be responsive to feedback whilst also not giving up or changing the 'big stuff' too easily or too soon. Plan and make sure that positive mental health promotion remains high profile with everyone and that the language of positive mental health is in common use.

In summary, this chapter has:

- explained the value of a whole-school approach to positive mental health promotion;
- outlined the importance of strong, knowledgeable school leadership to successful promotion;
- suggested how to include parents;
- presented ways to move forward with the findings of the audit;
- offered five frameworks for generating discussion and planning for positive mental health promotion.

It concludes that it takes time to develop an effective whole-school approach to positive mental health promotion that is compatible with the school ethos and values and that suits the needs of all involved.

9 Teacher wellbeing

This chapter discusses the literature and research on teacher wellbeing.

There is emphasis on the importance of teacher wellbeing to positive mental health promotion and the need for a school environment that promotes positive mental health for all those who work within the school. Suggestions are offered on how to promote staff wellbeing and ways to reduce stressors.

The evidence and theory

Teacher wellbeing depends on 'harmony' between the personal needs and expectations of a teacher and the environment, physical and emotional, in which they work (Bricheno, Brown and Lubansky, 2009).

Being a teacher promoting positive mental health is demanding and often stressful. For successful wellbeing promotion, it is necessary to identify and acknowledge the potentially detrimental impact on teacher wellbeing before beginning to address it. The positive wellbeing of teachers is fundamental to positive mental health promotion. Whilst this involves taking positive action to foster and maintain their own health, it also requires the support of school leadership and a supportive environment. Teachers need to feel that their emotional needs are being met.

It is important to recognise that positive mental health promotion, like teaching in general, is challenging and demanding (Gu and Day, 2013). Teachers make an emotional investment in promoting their pupils' wellbeing. In my most recent research, participants spoke of the toll that came from working hard to create the supportive ethos, to build positive relationships and to be a role model for the behaviours and characteristics related to positive mental health, not to mention the commitment and effort taken to overcome the challenges.

That teaching, and positive mental health promotion in particular, require such personal qualities and sensitive accountable judgement makes teachers vulnerable to the opinion and criticism of others (Hargreaves, 2016; Zembylas, 2011). Teachers may be acting in the best interests of the child, but as there can be no rigid framework to determine how to respond or how best to act in each unique situation, teacher judgement is scrutinised; teachers are expected to be able to explain and justify their actions (Biesta, 2016; Hargreaves, 2016). Such vulnerability is a further threat to teacher wellbeing (Kelchtermans, 2011).

Whilst positive experiences in the classroom can trigger feelings of pride, joy and job satisfaction in the teacher, less successful experiences have more of a detrimental impact and can lead to feelings of disappointment, guilt, anger or fear. Such work is similar to that of other caring professions and is often called emotional labour, the purpose of which is to make others feel that they are cared for and safe. Teachers contribute to the growth and happiness of their pupils, but they also need to have positive mental health for the good of education and for themselves. It should not be a matter of the teacher prioritising the needs of the child and the profession to the detriment of their own needs. In a healthy, caring relationship such as the teacher-pupil one, the teacher carer can benefit as much as the cared-for child. Thus, positive mental health promotion relies on the emotional and professional engagement of the teacher.

Emotional labour can increase job satisfaction, but it also brings its demands. The ability to form positive relationships is influenced by wellbeing. Relationships with pupils can enhance or impact negatively on teacher wellbeing. While teachers are getting something back from their care, this balances out the emotional demands (Noddings, 2011). It is when there is an imbalance of giving and receiving that emotional labour can be detrimental to wellbeing and, consequently, to the teacher's ability to promote positive mental health (Veldman et al., 2016). Spilt and Koomen (2009), believe that when a teacher has a positive relationship with pupils, they can cope better with incidences of poor behaviour. Although they might find such experiences stressful, they see them as worthwhile steps in a child's social or emotional development. If teachers value positive relationships and are consistently putting a great deal of effort into forming relationships with pupils to no effect, this can leave them feeling hurt, disenchanted and emotionally drained. In this way, disruptive behaviour in class is more stressful and more likely to lead to teacher burnout when it is from those pupils with whom, despite all their efforts, teachers have a troubled relationship (Split, Koomen and Thijs, 2011).

Such emotional exhaustion, a common feature of teacher stress, reduces teacher engagement in their relationships with pupils and can make them feel more negatively towards those pupils (Bomber, 2007; Han and Weiss, 2005; Lynn, McKay and Atkins, 2003). Negative emotions transmit from teacher to pupils (Bahman and Maffini, 2008; Rogers and Freiberg, 1994). Poor relationships between teacher and pupils have a negative impact on the classroom environment, which can lead to an increase in challenging behaviour in the classroom, causing yet more stress for the teacher and the pupils. In contrast, as previously noted, positive relationships between teacher and pupils can enhance pupil learning and social and emotional wellbeing. If teachers feel good about themselves, they are more likely to have the resilience to cope with challenges, and, in turn, their pupils benefit from having good role models for resilience (Adelman and Taylor, 2006; Gu and Day, 2007). However, teachers cannot serve as positive role models for emotional literacy nor offer the support the children need if they are burnt out or emotionally exhausted.

Teachers with optimism and a good sense of self-efficacy are less likely to suffer from high levels of stress because their increased confidence helps them maintain engagement with their pupils and their role. However, persistent emotional demands reduce teachers' feelings of efficacy and confidence and can make them anxious about carrying out the emotionally sensitive elements of positive mental health promotion (Han and Weiss, 2005).

Although positive relationships benefit the teacher as well as the pupils and emotional engagement with pupils is what enables teachers to carry out their role as teachers, to promote positive mental health, the teachers' needs must still be met so that they can flourish, fulfil their responsibilities and avoid burnout. A balance of giving and receiving is required so that the professional is able to care for others without unrealistic self-expectations, recognising their own limitations and taking steps to avoid stress and exhaustion. There should be recognition from policy makers and school leaders that, in order to care for others, the teacher must first care for self (Gu and Day, 2013; Higgins, 2011; Noddings, 2007).

There are significant external or environmental factors that impact on teacher wellbeing. Such factors are seen to be outside a teacher's control, yet having control over their work is considered important to wellbeing. Such external contributors to stress include:

- staff shortages,
- a lack of resources,
- rising pupil numbers,
- increasingly high workloads,
- the pressure of monitoring and accountability,
- frequent change of policy or expectations.

Teacher wellbeing and positive mental health promotion

Much can be learned from existing research into teacher wellbeing and evaluations of positive mental health promotion. When implementing a whole-school approach to positive mental health promotion, there should be opportunities for teachers to learn together. This increases the understanding of the facts and also helps to build greater emotional understanding through the strengthening of relationships with colleagues (Fullan, 2011; Hargreaves, 2016). The support that teachers gain from being in a professional learning community within their school can increase their resilience, their sense of belonging and their ability to cope with the demands of change (Gu and Day, 2013; Fullan, 2011; Nieto, 2003). In this way, it has the potential to increase positive teacher mental health. This, in turn, is more likely to increase the wellbeing and learning outcomes of the children in the school.

Positive mental health promotion is most effective when teachers and pupils are both working in a nonjudgemental climate. Teachers feel better able to develop professionally, to reflect, to ask for help and to build on their experiences. This again increases the teacher's ability to promote positive mental health. The challenges of the role can be offset significantly when there is a good team spirit amongst staff, who are able to share the burden with colleagues, to discuss solutions, or just to acknowledge the impact of their work on their wellbeing.

The absence of a supportive whole-school ethos is often the result of poor relationships with colleagues or a lack of support from senior management. The absence of support from colleagues is a significant contributor to teacher stress. It can reduce teacher confidence and their ability to carry out their responsibilities which reduces self- efficacy and is detrimental to teacher wellbeing. How can teachers promote social and emotional wellbeing effectively when they are working in a socially unhealthy climate? How can they model positive relationships if they do not have these with colleagues? Sometimes positive mental health promotion involves significant and challenging work with school staff to build relationships and strengthen bonds and team spirit.

When positive mental health promotion is not a whole-school priority, teachers can be put under pressure to prioritise other elements of their role; they might even be told not to waste valuable teaching time on what they see as practice fundamental to positive mental health. Children receive mixed messages, which further undermine the efforts of the teacher working to promote positive mental health.

The teacher's role in their wellbeing

A healthy approach would be one in which the teacher has some strategies and self-care routines to reduce or offset any risks to wellbeing. The teacher knows that they have some responsibility to manage their wellbeing but that they should be able to ask for help if the burden becomes too great. This balance recognises the teachers' role in their own wellbeing whilst acknowledging that the school also has a duty to safeguard teacher wellbeing.

At the unhealthy extreme, there can be a harmful acceptance or belief that being in a caring profession such as teaching requires self-sacrifice or altruism at the cost of personal care. The teacher can give up even trying to achieve a healthy work-life balance. This just begins a downward spiral in health.

In my recent research, teachers spoke of the many ways they tried to minimise the impact of pressure on a daily basis. Strategies for managing when they felt stressed during the school day included:

- deep breaths and calming thoughts,
- silent screams into a cupboard,
- bursting into song,
- having a moan in the staffroom,
- asking for help,
- eating cake,
- going for a run at lunch break,
- taking the whole class out for an impromptu quick five minutes exercise or play,
- acknowledging when something is not working and pausing,
- sharing emotions in a constructive way with pupils.

(See Chapter 5.)

Recommended strategies for staying well include:

- having a life outside school – playing netball, doing something that isn't work;
- trying not to take things personally;
- trying not to take worries home – mindfulness really helps;
- knowing you can't fix everything;

- yoga;
- laughing together;
- supporting each other;
- valuing yourself;
- having a sense of humour;
- sharing – if someone asks how you feel, you have to be honest;
- having social times;
- going to the gym three times a week;
- walking the dogs;
- getting support from friends and family;
- working in little groups and bringing in bars of chocolate or Friday scones;
- being able to come in the next day saying, 'That was yesterday. Each day starts again';
- safeguarding weekends and evenings as much as possible;
- celebrating success as a staff team and personally.

Alongside individual self-care and specific strategies such as these, there needs to be a culture where it is normal to talk about the importance of looking after your own wellbeing. There needs to be an emphasis on valuing and promoting teacher and staff wellbeing. Nobody should have to hide any steps they are taking to promote their own positive mental health for fear of negative judgement. Thus, the whole school culture is fundamental to individual teacher wellbeing.

The school's role in teacher wellbeing promotion

If a school is seeking to promote positive mental health, it needs to include within its action planning steps to promote staff wellbeing and remove or reduce threats. These actions may seem like the responsibility of school leadership, as indeed they are, but they are also the responsibility of everyone within the school. Everyone needs to look out for each other and be aware of their role in promoting staff wellbeing. As already suggested, there needs to be explicit valuing of teacher wellbeing, self-care and actions to promote their own and others' positive mental health. Health-promoting actions and discussions should be encouraged, and criticism or censure for prioritising health should not be tolerated. Working to promote emotional wellbeing in pupils is demanding and draining. Such aspects of the teacher's role should be acknowledged, with measures in place to offset them as part of the whole school culture. In summary, the school should seek to do the following:

- Develop a nonjudgemental professional learning community underpinned by mutual respect and valuing.
- Address the emotional needs of teachers (and the whole school staff). This might be done by first listening to colleagues to find out what the stressors and challenges are. The school should have a safe space for sharing concerns and talking through problems.
- Take time to check in with colleagues. Are they struggling? Put mechanisms in place for staff to raise concerns about their own or others' wellbeing.
- Value wellbeing promotion of staff as well as pupils.

- Build relationships and peer support networks.
- Give staff a voice – gather perspective, opinion, hopes and suggestions.
- Use some professional learning or INSET time to develop teacher resilience or emotional literacy – not how to teach it but to consider what emotional literacy and resilience look like in school and how to strengthen this capacity in themselves and each other.
- Listen to concerns – find ways to overcome them rather than accepting them.
- Make sure there is not an overt or hidden acceptance of long working hours, no personal time and the strains of teaching. Instead, make it acceptable and a strength to find ways to manage workload and wellbeing. Learn to say no and accept no as a reasonable response.
- Encourage staff to have self-care strategies. Sometimes this can be done through finding things that will nurture a whole school team, such as a spa day, but this only works if it does nurture everyone attending. Otherwise, an action intended to promote wellbeing can, in fact, reduce it for some. Offering optional sessions/social activities where there is no pressure to join in such as mindfulness classes, yoga and nights out can be just as effective.
- Remind colleagues of reasonable working hours. Suggest that they go home if they are working too late.

In summary, this chapter has:

- recognised the challenges of being a teacher;
- emphasised the importance of teacher wellbeing to positive mental health promotion;
- considered the teacher's role in their own wellbeing;
- emphasised the value of a positive, supportive climate for staff, making clear that the school has a responsibility to promote the wellbeing of all their staff and outlining ways to do this;
- presented strategies used by teachers to look after their wellbeing.

It concludes with the audit questions for school staff wellbeing.

Audit questions for school staff-teacher wellbeing

Do you know how to look after your mental health?
What do you do to look after your mental health?
Do you know what to do if your mental health is not good?
What support is there in school to promote your positive mental health?
How do you contribute to the positive mental health of colleagues?
How do colleagues contribute to your positive mental health?

Appendices

Appendix 1

Appendix 1

Audit for pupils – identifying strengths and needs	**Ethos**
What does it feel like to be in your classroom?	
Why does it feel this way?	
What things about your classroom or school make you feel good?	
What things about your classroom or school make you feel not so good?	
Do you always feel safe at school? Why?	
What kind of things make you feel safe at school?	
What kinds of things make you feel less safe at school?	
What do you do if you have a problem in class?	
Is there someone you would ask for help if you needed it?	

Appendix 2

Appendix 2

<table>
<tr><th colspan="3">Audit for pupils – identifying strengths and needs</th><th>Positive relationships</th></tr>
<tr><td colspan="3">In your class, do you have:</td><td></td></tr>
<tr><td>no friends</td><td>a few friends</td><td>lots of friends</td><td></td></tr>
<tr><td colspan="3">Would you like to have:</td><td></td></tr>
<tr><td>more friends</td><td>the same number of friends</td><td>fewer friends</td><td></td></tr>
<tr><td colspan="3">How do you show respect to others in your class?</td><td></td></tr>
<tr><td colspan="3">How do you show you are considerate of and care about other children in your class?</td><td></td></tr>
<tr><td colspan="3">How do you include others?</td><td></td></tr>
<tr><td colspan="3">What does valuing other children in your class look like?</td><td></td></tr>
<tr><td colspan="3">In what ways do you feel respected by other children in your class?</td><td></td></tr>
<tr><td colspan="3">In what ways do you feel considered/cared about by other children in your class?</td><td></td></tr>
<tr><td colspan="3">In what ways do you feel included by other children in your class?</td><td></td></tr>
<tr><td colspan="3">In what ways do you feel valued by other children in your class?</td><td></td></tr>
<tr><td colspan="3">How do you know how to behave in your classroom?</td><td></td></tr>
<tr><td colspan="3">Are there things about other children's behaviour that make you feel good?</td><td></td></tr>
<tr><td colspan="3">Are there things about other children's behaviour that make you feel not so good?</td><td></td></tr>
<tr><td colspan="3">How does your teacher help you get on with the others in your classroom?</td><td></td></tr>
<tr><td colspan="3">Do you have someone in your classroom that you trust to help you if you are unhappy or if you have a problem? Who?</td><td></td></tr>
<tr><td colspan="3">Is there anything else you would like to say about friendships and getting on with other children in your class?</td><td></td></tr>
</table>

Appendix 3

Appendix 3

Audit for pupils – identifying strengths and needs	Emotional literacy
Do the children in the classroom talk about how they feel? If so, please give an example.	
Are you encouraged to talk about your feelings?	
Does it feel safe to talk about feelings in your classroom?	
What makes it feel safe or unsafe to talk about feelings?	
Does your teacher talk about her/his feelings?	
Does your teacher talk about the feelings of children in the class?	
Does your teacher teach you about feelings?	
Do you talk about the feelings of characters in fiction (stories/poems/films/TV)?	
What do you do at school if you feel:	*You might do lots of different things.*
angry	
worried	
happy	
scared	
jealous	
excited	
proud	
embarrassed	
sorry	
miserable	
uncertain or unsettled	

Appendix 4

Appendix 4

Audit for pupils – identifying strengths and needs	Empowering children as learners
Empowering children as learners	
Do you have time to think about how your learning is going?	
Do you know how to reflect on a task you have done?	
Do you know how you learn or how you learn best?	
Thinking of **how** you work, not **what** you do, please answer the following:	
What kinds of learning do you find easy?	
What kinds of learning do you find difficult?	
How do you know when you have done well?	
What do you do when you find something difficult?	
Do you know what your next steps in learning are in any subject?	
Can you talk about your strengths and next steps in learning?	
What do you do when you have achieved a development need?	

Appendix 5

Appendix 5

Audit for pupils - identifying strengths and needs	Teaching and understanding
Do you learn about emotional health or mental health at school?	
What kinds of things do you do?	
Do you know what mental health is?	
Describe someone with good mental health.	
Describe someone with poor mental health.	
Do you know how to look after your mental health?	
Do you know what to do if your mental health is not good?	
What lessons in school do you think are meant to help you understand mental health?	
What support is there in school to help you have good mental health?	
What support is there in school to help you if you are worried about your mental health?	

Appendix 6

Appendix 6

Audit for school staff – identifying strengths and needs	Ethos
What does it feel like to work in your school?	
Why might this be?	
Is there anything that could be improved about the school ethos/ environment to make it feel a better place to work? If so, what could be done? What would make it feel a better place to work?	
Do you have colleagues you trust to confide in?	
Do you feel supported in your role? Why?	
What would make you feel more supported?	
Classroom ethos	
What does it feel like to be in your classroom?	
Why?	
Do you know how the children feel about their classroom?	
Thinking of the physical environment:	
Which aspects do you think contribute to creating a safe and positive ethos?	
Which aspects might make it a less safe or positive ethos?	
Thinking of the social and emotional environment:	
Which elements do you think contribute to a positive ethos?	
Which elements detract from a positive ethos?	
How often do the children smile and laugh in the classroom?	
Do the children look relaxed/content/secure?	
How do the children treat each other?	
How well do the children collaborate?	
Do the children show respect to each other and to you?	
Do the children show care for others? How?	
Do the children express concerns or difficulties?	

Appendix 7

Appendix 7

Audit for school staff – identifying strengths and needs	Positive relationships
Are there any children who have difficulty making friends? How do you know?	
What steps do you take to promote positive relationships?	
What is your role in the children's development of social skills and positive relationships?	
How well prepared do you feel for this role? Do you have any training needs?	
What things about the children's interactions and relationships with each other and with you contribute to a positive ethos?	
What things about the children's interactions and relationships with each other and with you detract from a positive ethos?	
Do relationship issues (arguments, bullying, disagreements etc.) interrupt the flow of the classroom? How often? What are the issues? What might be causing these issues?	
Do you take time to reflect on the children's social skills that contribute to a positive ethos?	
Which skills that you or the children have contribute to a positive ethos?	
What direct teaching of social and relationship skills do you do? How is this reinforced in practice?	
What specific needs do the children have that might contribute to or detract from their ability to form positive relationships?	

Appendix 8

Appendix 8

Audit for school staff – identifying strengths and needs	Emotional literacy
Do the children in the classroom talk about how they feel? If so, please give an example.	
Are children encouraged to talk about their feelings?	
What do you do to makes children feel safe talking about their feelings?	
Do you ever talk about your feelings? Give an example, or say why if you do not.	
Do you talk about the feelings of the children in the class?	
What direct teaching of emotional literacy do you do?	
Are you emotionally literate?	
Do you model emotional literacy? Give an example.	
Would you like more training or support with emotional literacy development?	

Appendix 9

Appendix 9

Audit for school staff – identifying strengths and needs	Empowering children as learners
Do you provide opportunities for children to reflect on their learning? Give examples.	
Do you help children develop the skills they need to reflect meaningfully on their learning? If so, give examples; if not, say why.	
What steps do you take to empower children as learners/ help them engage meaningfully in self-evaluation and target setting?	
Are these successful?	
How could these be more successful?	

Appendix 10

Appendix 10

Audit for school staff – identifying strengths and needs	Teaching and learning
Do you have a secure understanding of positive mental health? How would you define it?	
What might a child with positive mental health be like?	
What might a child with poor mental health be like?	
Do you teach children about emotional health or mental health?	
What kinds of things do you do?	
What explicit teaching do you do related to the many elements of positive mental health promotion?	
What embedded practice do you have in place to promote positive mental health?	

Appendix 11

Appendix 11

Audit for school staff - identifying strengths and needs	Teacher wellbeing
Do you know how to look after your mental health?	
What do you do to look after your mental health?	
Do you know what to do if your mental health is not good?	
What support is there in school to promote your positive mental health?	
How do you contribute to the positive mental health of colleagues?	
How do colleagues contribute to your positive mental health?	

Appendix 12

Appendix 12

Audit strengths overview

Framework for using the audit results for development planning in positive mental health promotion

Element of audit	Top 3 development needs identified through staff audit	Top 3 development needs identified through pupil audit
Ethos 1		
Ethos 2		
Ethos 3		
Positive relationships 1		
Positive relationships 2		
Positive relationships 3		
Emotional literacy 1		
Emotional literacy 2		
Emotional literacy 3		
Empowering children 1		
Empowering children 2		
Empowering children 3		
Teaching & understanding 1		
Teaching & understanding 2		
Teaching & understanding 3		
Staff wellbeing 1		
Staff wellbeing 2		
Staff wellbeing 3		

Appendix 13

Appendix 13

Audit development needs overview

Element of audit	Top 3 strengths identified through staff audit	Top 3 strengths identified through pupil audit
Ethos 1		
Ethos 2		
Ethos 3		
Positive relationships 1		
Positive relationships 2		
Positive relationships 3		
Emotional literacy 1		
Emotional literacy 2		
Emotional literacy 3		
Empowering children 1		
Empowering children 2		
Empowering children 3		
Teaching & understanding 1		
Teaching & understanding 2		
Teaching & understanding 3		
Staff wellbeing 1		
Staff wellbeing 2		
Staff wellbeing 3		

Professional learning appendices 14–21

The following appendices present the professional learning activities from Chapter 8 in photocopiable format.

Appendix 14

Appendix 14

Professional learning 1: mental health understanding part 1 - discussion activity for school staff

Small-group activity: the audit asks the following questions. Discuss your own answers with colleagues, exploring any differences and the potential reasons for these:

a) Do you have a secure understanding of positive mental health?
b) How would you define it?
c) What might a child with positive mental health be like?
d) What might a child with poor mental health be like?

Follow up as whole group

a) Explore confidence levels. What level of understanding of positive mental health is there? There are so many misconceptions around that it is understandable to feel uncertain or to lack confidence in the concept of positive mental health. For those staff who wish to increase their understanding of positive mental health, Chapter 1 of this book is recommended reading. It also signposts you to further readings if required.
b) Shared understanding. Gather the various perspectives of positive mental health and try to come to an agreed, whole-school definition of what positive mental health is.
c) Shared understanding. In the same way, now collect characteristics of a child with positive mental health. Can these be represented pictorially? This is also an activity that can be carried out with children.
d) Shared understanding. What are the many and varying characteristics of a child with poor mental health? Now think of the school itself. What kinds of mental health difficulties are present? What challenges to the children's mental health do they experience in their lives? Is there anything that leaps out as a priority for targeted strategies?

Additional small-group task: Ask small groups to talk about the stigma associated with mental health. Is there a fear of the term? Is the word 'mental' used as an insult or deficit adjective in the school? Do any colleagues believe that mental health is not part of their remit?

Additional whole-group follow-up: What challenges might we face in this school in relation to understanding mental health, community understanding and valuing of the terms and concept of positive mental health promotion? Do any immediately necessary actions become apparent?

Remember, positive mental health promotion is for all children, but some children might have particular challenges or be at risk of specific threats to mental health. Such children will benefit from the whole-school positive mental health promotion approaches, but effective promotion also includes removing risks to mental health, and this sometimes involves targeted strategies or specific small-group teaching in addition to the whole-school approaches. This is not to be confused with specific support for poor mental health, which may be offered by mental health specialists.

By the end of this first session, there should be agreement on the school definition of positive mental health promotion and what a child with positive mental health might look like and identification of threats and risks to mental health experienced by children in the school. It may feel like you have done nothing but talk, but coming to a shared understanding and exploring attitudes, fears and perspectives is a crucial foundation for whole-school consistency.

Appendix 15

Appendix 15

Professional learning 2: mental health understanding part 2 - discussion activity for school staff

Small-group activity: the audit asks the questions repeated below. Discuss your own answers with colleagues, exploring any differences and the potential reasons for these:

a) Do you teach children about emotional health or mental health?
b) What kinds of things do you do?
c) What explicit teaching do you do related to the many elements of positive mental health promotion?
d) What embedded practice do you have in place to promote positive mental health?

In this session, the aim is to get mixed groups of school staff to talk about what they already do and to tease out their understanding of embedded versus discrete positive mental health promotion.

Gather perspectives from the individual group discussions with the whole room and then give groups a scenario to discuss:

Scenario 1

The children in Alison's class are eight years old. They cannot work together without arguments. Alison has plans for group science activities and paired writing, but the children spend their time arguing, and the science or writing does not get done. Alison does not want a silent classroom where children work alone, so she decides to take time out from other lessons each day to work on collaboration.

She starts with lessons on what makes a good friend, how to work with a partner and what to do if there is a disagreement. She tries these lessons for a week and then returns to her plans for collaborative study. What embedded wellbeing promotion needs to be in place for the targeted lessons on collaboration and friendship to move from conceptual to lived? How does she support the children to move from talking about a good partner or friend to actually being one?

Scenario 2

Rob has a class of ten-year-olds. Whenever he gives them open-ended tasks or activities designed to challenge their thinking and problem solving, they end up lining up by his desk asking for help because they are frightened to get it wrong. They miss the security of a set method leading to a right answer.

Rob has read a lot on mindset and decides to introduce some specific sessions on mindset, daring to try and learning from mistakes. What does he need to do to embed and reinforce these messages into his daily practice?

Discussion

There are no correct answers to this as every classroom and school will be different, but what we are working towards is a greater understanding of how what the teacher does all day every day reinforces and models the specific areas of social, emotional and mental wellbeing targeted in the discrete lessons.

Key messages we hope to come from the discussions are:

- growing understanding of the need for more than just a set of discrete lessons;
- teacher as model;
- consistent expectation;
- praise when children enact and embody the healthy characteristics sought (good friendship, conflict resolution etc.);
- support, examples and reminders of (for example) positive behaviour or positive attitude around the room to help children;
- avoidance of mixed messages – do not tolerate the undesired characteristics; instead use positive reinforcement.

Appendix 16

Appendix 16

Assessing social wellbeing - developing staff understanding

Discuss in groups:

- What skills, behaviours and attitudes would you expect a child to display?
- Target specific elements of social wellbeing.
- Draw up success criteria (SC) (as class/group and individual).
- Teach children how to evaluate self and others according to the target SC. Teach them how to give and receive feedback. (This is a social skill to develop a social skill.)

Share discussions in the whole room, then each group should carry out the next task using the learning activities in the box as a context and the image as a framework.

- Try it now - develop social SC for group activity.
- You will have your core subject SC; what social skills are necessary to the task?
- How will you know a child has demonstrated these skills?
- How will they be evaluated?
- What constructive feedback could be used?

Contexts for the social skill SC task

Predict and explore which materials float and which sink.
Set up a simple circuit to make a bulb light up.
Design or create a poster or advert for a new snack.
Discuss and summarise a chapter of group text.

Good teamwork

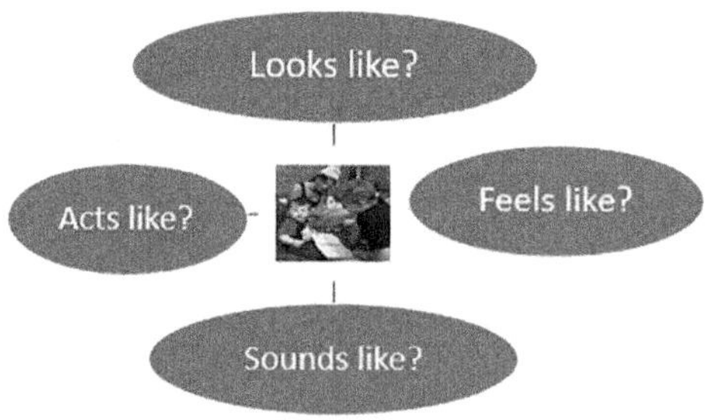

Appendix 17

Appendix 17

Unpicking ethos – group task 1

This might be a useful way to move forwards with a health-promoting ethos if that is the area of promotion identified as a development priority.

Group task 1: Give each group one of the following aspects of ethos:

- safe,
- respecting,
- supportive,
- inclusive.

1 Ask each group to consider what they do to make the school feel like the characteristic they have been given.
2 Collect three key actions or policies per group.
3 Now look at the pupil responses to the questions about ethos.
4 How does what the staff has identified match what the children say?
5 Give an opportunity for groups to discuss whether they want to change their key actions in line with pupil responses.
6 Discuss: does everyone have and understand their roles in positive mental health promotion?

Appendix 18

Appendix 18

Unpicking ethos - group task 2

Each group should be allocated a different characteristic of a health-promoting ethos:

- sense of belonging,
- acceptance,
- encouraging and rewarding positive behaviour,
- encouraging and praising positive social interaction.

Look at the pupil responses on what makes the school feel not such a good place to be.

In relation to their allocated characteristic, each group should discuss:

- priorities for change,
- positives on which to build.

Do any next steps or development needs stand out?

Homework task

In between tasks 2 and 3, it would be helpful for those attending the professional learning sessions to have a day or a week to be thinking specifically about ethos as they carry out their daily work in school and as they move through different parts of the school. Each member of staff could be responsible for concentrating on a specific element to observe and gather more information. Individual practitioner enquiry tasks could bring valuable insight and understanding to the positive mental health promotion development process.

Appendix 19

Appendix 19

Unpicking ethos - whole-school professional learning

Group task 3

Look at the remaining characteristics of a health-promoting environment and evaluate where they think each class or the whole school does well or could do better.

Ethos characteristic	Strengths	Areas for development
prohibiting discrimination and promoting equality		
fostering positive relationships between staff, pupils and families		
engendering in children a sense of security and achievement		
empowering children		
giving children a valued voice in school decisions		
encouraging and rewarding healthy behaviours in addition to academic achievement		
praise and positive feedback		
having emotionally literate teachers		
providing social and emotional support for those within it		
ensuring the school is physically in good repair with fit-for-purpose fittings and furniture		

Combine these with results of tasks 1 and 2:

Ethos characteristic	Strengths	Areas for development
Safe		
Respecting		
Supportive		
Inclusive		
Ethos characteristic	**Strengths**	**Areas for development**
Sense of belonging		
Acceptance		
Encouraging and rewarding positive behaviour		
Encouraging and praising positive social interaction		

Now consider the following questions:

1. What are the strengths of different parts of the school and the school as a whole?
2. Are there any school priorities?
3. How do children feel being in the school?
4. What friendships and relationships do the children like?
5. What social elements do the children dislike?
6. Is there consistency across the children's responses?
7. If not, where are the differences? Is there any pattern? How can we find out why there are differences?
8. How do we feel to work here? What is it like to be here?
9. In this school, what do we want it to feel like to be a pupil and a teacher?
10. How can we achieve this?
11. How do we gather pupil perspective on this?

Use the discussion and teacher and pupil responses to draw up a plan for next steps or a whole-school health-promoting ethos development plan.

Appendix 20

Appendix 20

Planning meaningful connections between discrete teaching and embedded promotion

Positive mental health promotion may include discrete lessons on a range of capacities or issues such as:

Specific emotions such as excitement	Making friends
Fear	Resolving arguments and friendship problems
Jealousy	Bullying
Happiness	Valuing self
Enthusiasm	Looking after self (personal safety)
Pride	Resilience
Anger	Positive mindset
Sex education	Peer pressure

Group task

Give each group a theme from the school positive mental health promotion scheme or curriculum planner or use themes from the list in Appendix 20. Gather ideas on how you would do the following for the allocated theme:

1 Identify all the times in the school day, week or year when such a characteristic is likely to occur.
2 Plan ways in which to make explicit the connections between the learning and school life.
3 Plan how the focus will be reinforced and praised during the whole day (outside the discrete lesson).
4 Identify links between the theme and the school vision or school policies.
5 Consider who else in the school will be with a child when they may experience this, such as lunchtime staff, PE specialists etc., and find ways to share plans and rationales with them.
6 Consider links to home life and ways to include parents within the theme.

Health promotion theme:	
Task	**Comments**
When might this theme occur in the school day? (e.g. jealousy at playtime, resilience in maths)	
How can you make explicit the connection between the lesson and the theme when it occurs during each day?	
How can the theme be recognised, praised and positively reinforced during each day?	
What are the links between the theme and the school vision or school policies?	
Who else in the school will be with a child when they may experience this? How can you share plans and rationales with them?	
What are the links to life outside school? How can parents be included?	

Appendix 21

Appendix 21

Planning whole-school positive mental health promotion

Having looked at specific elements of the audit, it is useful now to consider staff and pupil responses across the whole audit in relation to the existing school vision and aims.

Discuss vision and aims

1. What are the whole-school vision and aims?
2. What healthy characteristics promote this vision?
3. Are any aspects of this vision likely to demote positive mental health?

With the responses to these three questions about vision and aims in mind, look at all the responses from pupils and the perspectives of school staff and carry out next task.

Look at the key elements of successful positive mental health promotion below:

Element	Comments
Consistent message	
Lived experience	
Relationship expectations	
Collective focus (e.g. on resilience or I can)	
Endorsing and reinforcing what happens in the classroom throughout the school	

Come to a shared agreement on:

Key points	Comments
What these elements should look like in this school	
How they might be achieved	
Any staff development needs	
Any staff support or wellbeing needs	
Any specific child mental health promotion needs or risks that have to be addressed for successful positive mental health promotion.	
How to work with the whole community	
Identifying the support (if any) needed from outside agencies	

Identify what should be in the consistent health-promoting messages permeating the school. Ensure that it is consistent with the school vision and aims or that steps are in place to adapt the vision and aims to be more compatible with positive mental health promotion.

References

Adelman, H. S. and Taylor, L. (2006) Mental health in schools and public health. *Public Health Reports Association of Schools of Public Health*, Vol.121:3, pp. 294–298.

Adelman, H. S. and Taylor, L. (2010) *Engaging learners, preventing problems, and improving schools*. Corwin: Sage Publications.

Bahman, S. and Maffini, H. (2008) *Developing children's emotional intelligence*. New York: Continuum International Publications.

Banerjee, R. (2010) Social and emotional aspects of learning in schools: Contributions to improving attainment, behaviour, and attendance. In *A report on data from the National Strategies Tracker School Project*. Sussex: Sussex University.

Benekos, P. (2016) How to be a good teacher: Passion, person, and pedagogy. *Journal of Criminal Justice Education*, Vol.27:2, pp. 1–13.

Bennathan, M. and Boxall, M. (2000) *Effective intervention in primary schools: Nurture groups*. London: Fulton.

Bielsa, V., Braddick, F., Jané-Llopis, E., Jenkins, R. and Puras, D. (2010) Child and adolescent mental health policies, programmes and infrastructures across Europe. *International Journal of Mental Health Promotion*, Vol.12:4, pp. 10–26.

Biesta, G. (2016) Good education and the teacher: Reclaiming educational professionalism. In J. Evers and R. Kneyber (Eds.), *Flip the system: Changing education from the ground up*. Abingdon, Oxon: Routledge. pp. 79–90.

Bomber, L. (2007) *Inside I'm hurting*. London: Worth Publishing.

Bradshaw, P. and Tipping, S. (2010) *Growing up in Scotland: Children's social, emotional and behavioural characteristics at entry to primary school*. Scottish Centre for Social Research. Edinburgh: The Scottish Government.

Bricheno, P., Brown, S. and Lubansky, R. (2009) *Teacher wellbeing: A review of the evidence*. London: Teacher Support Network.

Bullough, R. (2011) Hope, happiness, teaching, and learning. In C. Day and J. Lee (Eds.), *New understandings of teacher's work emotions and educational change*. New York: Springer. pp. 15–30.

Cooper, B. (2010) In search of profound empathy in learning relationships: Understanding the mathematics of moral learning environments. *Journal of Moral Education*, Vol.39:1, pp. 79–99.

Cushman, P., Clelland, T. and Hornby, G. (2011) Health-promoting schools and mental health issues: A survey of New Zealand schools. *Pastoral Care in Education*, Vol.29, pp. 247–260.

Denzin, N. (1984) *On understanding emotion*. San Francisco: Jossey-Bass.

Dweck, C. (2017) *Mindset-updated edition: Changing the way you think to fulfil your potential*. New York: Ballantine Books.

Ekornes, S., Hauge, T. and Lund, I. (2012) Teachers as mental health promoters: A study of teachers' understanding of the concept of mental health. *International Journal of Mental Health Promotion*, Vol.14, pp. 289–310.

Elsley, S. and McMellon, C. (2010) *Doing ok? Children and Young People's views on what affects their mental health*. Edinburgh: Centre for Research on Families and Relationships.

Folkman, S. and Moskowitz, J. (2000) Positive affect and the other side of coping. *American Psychologist*, Vol.55, pp. 647–654.

Fredrickson, B. and Joiner, T. (2002) Positive emotions trigger upward spirals toward emotional wellbeing. *Psychological Science*, Vol.13:2, pp. 172–175.

Fullan, M. (2011) *The six secrets of change: What the best leaders do to help their organizations survive and thrive*. San Francisco: Jossey-Bass.

Goroshit, M. and Hen, M. (2016) Teachers' empathy: Can it be predicted by self-efficacy? *Teachers and Teaching*, Vol.22:7, pp. 805–818.

Green, J., Howes, F., Waters, E., Maher, E. and Oberklaid, F. (2005) Promoting the social and emotional health of primary school-aged children: Reviewing the evidence base for school based interventions. *International Journal of Mental Health Promotion*, Vol.7:3, pp. 30–36.

Greenberg, M., Weissberg, R., O'Brien, M., Fredericks, L., Elias, M. and Resnik, H. (2003) Enhancing school-based prevention and youth development through coordinated social, emotional, and academic learning. *American Psychologist*, Vol.58, pp. 466–474.

Gu, Q. and Day, C. (2007) Teachers' resilience: A necessary condition for effectiveness. *Teaching and Teacher Education*, Vol.23, pp. 1302–1316.

Gu, Q. and Day, C. (2013) Challenges to teacher resilience. *British Educational Research Journal*, Vol.39:1, pp. 22–44.

Hall, S. (2010) Supporting mental health and wellbeing at a whole-school level: Listening to and acting upon children's views. *Emotional and Behavioural Difficulties*, Vol.15:4, pp. 323–339.

Hallam, S. (2009) An evaluation of the Social and Emotional Aspects of Learning (SEAL) programme: Promoting positive behaviour, effective learning and well-being in primary school children. *Oxford Review of Education*, Vol.35:3, pp. 313–330.

Han, S. and Weiss, B. (2005) Sustainability of teacher implementation of school-based mental health programs. *Journal of Abnormal Child Psychology*, Vol.33:6, pp. 665–679.

Hargreaves, A. (2005) Educational change takes ages: Life, career and generational factors in teachers' emotional responses to educational change. *Teaching and Teacher Education*, Vol.21, pp. 967–983.

Hargreaves, A. (2016) Autonomy and transparency: Two good ideas gone bad. In J. Evers and R. Kneyber (Eds.), *Flip the system changing education from the ground up*. Abingdon, UK: Routledge. pp. 120–133.

Hattie, J. (2012) *Visible learning for teachers: Maximizing impact on learning*. Abingdon, UK: Routledge.

Herrman, H., Saxena, S. and Moodie, R. (2005) *Promoting mental health: Concepts, emerging evidence, practice: A report of the World Health Organization, Department of Mental Health and Substance Abuse in collaboration with the Victorian Health Promotion Foundation and the University of Melbourne*. Geneva: WHO Press. p. 258.

Higgins, C. (2011) *The good life of teaching: An ethics of professional practice*. Oxford: Wiley Blackwell.

Holt, D. (2019) *The Primary School Teacher's Responsibility to Promote Positive Mental Health*. University of Edinburgh thesis.

Hornby, G. and Atkinson, M. (2003) A framework for promoting mental health in school. *Pastoral Care in Education: An International Journal of Personal, Social and Emotional Development*, Vol.21, pp. 3–9.

Humphrey, N. (2004) Facilitating a positive sense of self in pupils with dyslexia: The role of teachers and peers. *Support for Learning*, Vol.18, pp. 129–136.

Kelchtermans, G. (2011) Vulnerability in teaching: The moral and political roots of a structural condition. In C. Day and J. Lee (Eds.), *New understandings of teacher's work emotions and educational change*. New York: Springer. pp. 65–82.

Kelly, B., Longbottom, J., Potts, F. and Williamson, J. (2004) Applying emotional intelligence: Exploring the PATHS curriculum. *Educational Psychology in Practice*, Vol.20, pp. 221–240.

Keyes, C. (2002) The mental health continuum: From languishing to flourishing in life. *Journal of Health and Social Behaviour*, Vol.43, pp. 207–222.

Luthar, S., Cicchetti, D. and Becker, B. (2000) The construct of resilience: A critical evaluation and guidelines for future work. *Child Development*, Vol.71:3, pp. 543–562.

Lynn, C., McKay, M. and Atkins, M. (2003) School social work: Meeting the mental health needs of students through collaboration with teachers. *Children & Schools*, Vol.25:4, pp. 197–209.

Mayer, D. (2011) "But that's the thing: Who else is going to teach besides the idealist?" Learning to teach in emotional contexts. In C. Day and J. Lee (Eds.), *New understandings of teacher's work emotions and educational change*. New York: Springer. pp. 137–150.

Mental Health Foundation (2016) *Relationships in the 21st century*. London: MHF.

Milkie, M. A. and Warner, C. H. (2011) Classroom learning environments and the mental health of first grade children. *Journal of Health and Social Behaviour*, Vol.52, pp. 4–22.

Morris, E. and Scott, C. (2003) *Whole school emotional literacy indicator*. Frampton on Severn: School of Emotional Literacy Publishing.

Murphy, R. (2016) *SPICe briefing child and adolescent mental health: Trends and key issues*. Edinburgh: SPICe Scottish Parliament Information Centre.

Murray, C. and Pianta, R. (2007) The importance of teacher-student relationships for adolescents with high incidence disabilities. *Theory into Practice*, Vol.46, pp. 105–112.

National Institute for Health and Clinical Excellence (2008) *Promoting children's social and emotional wellbeing in primary education*. London: NICE.

Newman, T. and Blackburn, S. (2002) *Transitions in the lives of children and young people: Resilience factors*. Edinburgh: Scottish Executive.

Nieto, S. (2003) *What keeps teachers going?* New York: Teachers College Press.

Noddings, N. (2007) Caring as relation and virtue in teaching. In R. Walker and P. Ivanhoe (Eds.), *Working virtue: Virtue ethics and contemporary moral problems*. New York: Oxford University Press. pp. 40–60.

Noddings, N. (2011) Stories and affect in teacher education: Nel Noddings' new understandings of teacher's work. In C. Day and J. Lee (Eds.), *New understandings of teacher's work emotions and educational change*. New York: Springer. pp. 151–163.

Office for National Statistics (ONS) (2015) *Insights into children's mental health and wellbeing*. London: Crown Copyright Office for National Statistics.

Oldfield, J., Humphrey, N. and Hebron, J. (2016) The role of parental and peer attachment relationships and school connectedness in predicting adolescent mental health outcomes. *Child and Adolescent Mental Health*, Vol.21:1, pp. 21–29.

Pantić, N. and Wubbels, T. (2012) Teachers' moral values and their interpersonal relationships with students and cultural competence. *Teaching and Teacher Education*, Vol.28:3, pp. 451–460.

Perry, L., Lennie, C. and Humphrey, N. (2008) Emotional literacy in the primary classroom: Teacher perceptions and practices. *Education 3-13: International Journal of Primary, Elementary and Early Years Education*, Vol.36:1, pp. 27–37.

Rogers, C. (1967) *On becoming a person: A therapist's view of psychotherapy*. London: Constable.

Rogers, C. (1980) *A way of being*. New York: Houghton Mifflin Company.

Rogers, C. and Freiberg, H. (1994) *Freedom to learn*. New York: Merrill Rothman and McMillan's (2003).

Rothman, S. and McMillan, J. (2003) Research report 36: Influences on achievement in literacy and numeracy: Longitudinal studies of Australian youth. Available online at: www.acer.edu.au/research/projects/say/research.html (accessed 20 April 2017).

Ryan, R. and Deci, E. (2001) On happiness and human potentials: A review of research on hedonic and eudaimonic well-being. *Annual Review of Psychology*, Vol.52, pp. 141–166.

Silverman, M. (2012) Virtue ethics, care ethics, and "the good life of teaching". *Action, Criticism, and Theory for Music Education*, Vol.11:2, pp. 96–122.

Spilt, J. and Koomen, H. (2009) Widening the view on teacher-child relationships: Teachers' narratives concerning disruptive versus non-disruptive children. *School Psychology Review*, Vol.38, pp. 86–101.

Split, J., Koomen, H. and Thijs, J. (2011) Teacher wellbeing: The importance of teacher-student relationships. *Educational Psychology Review*, Vol.23:4, pp. 457–477.

Tarrant, P. and Holt, D. (2016) *Metacognition in the primary classroom*. Abingdon, UK: Routledge.

Thompson, E. (2007) *Mind in life*. Cambridge, MA: Harvard University Press.

Veldman, I., Admiraal, W., van Tartwijk, J., Mainhard, T. and Wubbels, T. (2016) Veteran teachers' job satisfaction as a function of personal demands and resources in the relationships with their students. *Teachers and Teaching Theory and Practice*, Vol.22:8, pp. 913–926.

Walberg, H., Zins, J. and Weissberg, R. (2004) Recommendations and conclusions: Implications for practice, training, research and policy. In J. Zins, R. Weissberg, M. Wang and H. Walberg (Eds.), *Building academic success on social and emotional learning*. New York: Teachers College Press. pp. 209–217.

Weare, K. (2010) *Developing the emotionally literate school*. London: Sage Publications.

World Health Organisation (1998) *Health promotion evaluation: Recommendations to Policymakers*. WHO Regional Office for Europe. Copenhagen: WHO.

World Health Organization (2001) *Mental health: New understanding, new hope*. The World Health Report. Geneva: WHO.

Wright, M., Banerjee, R., Hoek, W., Rieffe, C. and Novin, S. (2010) Depression and social anxiety in children: Differential links with coping strategies. *Journal of Abnormal Child Psychology*, Vol.38:3, pp. 405–419.

Zeidner, M., Roberts, R. and Matthews, G. (2002) Can emotional intelligence be schooled? A critical review. *Educational Psychologist*, Vol.37, pp. 215–231.

Zembylas, M. (2011) Teaching and teacher emotions: A post-structural perspective. In C. Day and J. Lee (Eds.), *New understandings of teacher's work emotions and educational change*. New York: Springer. pp. 31–43.

Zins, J., Weissberg, R., Wang, M. and Walberg, H. (2004) *Building academic success on social and emotional learning*. New York: Teachers College Press.

Index

Note: Page numbers in *italics* indicate figures.